ACCA

PRACTICE & REVISION KIT

Paper 2.3

Business Taxation

FA 2002

For June and December 2003 exams

BPP Professional Education
January 2003

First edition April 2001
Third edition January 2003

ISBN 0 7517 0761 9 (previous edition 0 7517 0515 2)

British Library Cataloguing-in-Publication Data
A catalogue record for this book
is available from the British Library

Published by

BPP Professional Education
Aldine House, Aldine Place
London W12 8AW

www.bpp.com

Printed in Great Britain by Ashford Colour Press

We are grateful to the Association of Chartered Certified Accountants for permission to reproduce past examination questions. The answers to the past examination questions have been prepared by BPP Professional Education.

The headings indicate the main topics of questions, but questions often cover several different topics.

Preparation questions, listed in italics, are followed by guidance notes. These notes show you how to approach the question, and thus ease the transition from study to examination practice.

Pilot paper questions for this syllabus are clearly indicated.

Question and answer checklist/index

BPP PROFESSIONAL EDUCATION

TOPIC INDEX

Listed below are the key Paper 2.3 syllabus topics and the numbers of the questions in this Kit covering those topics.

If you need to concentrate your practice and revision on certain topics or if you want to attempt all available questions that refer to a particular subject (be they preparation or exam-standard) you will find this index useful.

Syllabus topic	Question numbers
Schedule D adjustments	1, 2, 3, 4, 11, 28, 37
Capital allowances	6, 7, 8, 9, 10, 11, 18, 37, 38, 51, 52, 58, 59
Computation of corporation tax	5, 6, 7, 8, 9, 16, 17, 18, 19, 20, 22, 51, 58
Payment of corporation tax	7, 8, 18, 23, 58
Company losses	12, 13, 51
Capital gains	8, 14, 15, 38, 39, 40, 41, 52, 54, 61
Overseas (corporate)	16, 17, 18, 55
Groups of companies	19, 20, 21, 62
Self-assessment for companies	22
Self-assessment for individuals	26, 27, 64
VAT	24, 25, 42, 53, 60
Income tax basis periods	28, 29, 30, 31, 32, 33, 37, 38, 57
Pensions	34, 35, 36
Income tax computations	35, 36, 37, 38, 39, 52, 59, 64
Employees	43, 44, 45, 46, 47, 52, 57, 59, 63
Income tax losses	29, 30, 33, 57
Partnerships	31, 32, 33
Tax planning	47, 48, 49, 50, 56, 63

EFFECTIVE REVISION

What you must remember

Effective use of time as you approach the exam is very important. You must remember:

> **Believe in yourself**
> **Use time sensibly**

Believe in yourself

Are you cultivating the right attitude of mind? There is absolutely no reason why you should not pass this exam if you adopt the correct approach.

- **Be confident** – you've passed exams before, you can pass them again
- **Be calm** – plenty of adrenaline but no panicking
- **Be focused** – commit yourself to passing the exam

Use time sensibly

1   **How much study time do you have?** Remember that you must **eat, sleep**, and of course, **relax**.

2   **How will you split that available time between each subject?** A **revision timetable**, covering **what** and **how** you will revise, will help you organise your revision effectively.

3   **What is your learning style?** AM/PM? Little and often/long sessions? Evenings/weekends?

4   **Do you have quality study time?** Unplug the phone. Let everybody know that you're studying and shouldn't be disturbed.

5   **Are you taking regular breaks?** Most people absorb more if they do not attempt to study for long uninterrupted periods of time. A five minute break every hour (to make coffee, watch the news headlines) can make all the difference.

6   Are you **rewarding yourself** for your hard work? Are you leading a **healthy lifestyle**?

What to revise

Key topics

You need to spend most time on, and practise full questions on, **key topics**.

> Key topics
> - Recur regularly
> - Underpin whole paper
> - Appear often in compulsory questions
> - Discussed currently in press
> - Covered in recent articles by examiner
> - Shown as high priority in study material
> - Tipped by lecturer

> **Difficult areas**

You may also still find certain areas of the syllabus difficult.

> Difficult areas
>
> - Areas you find dull or pointless
> - Subjects you highlighted as difficult when taking notes
> - Topics that gave you problems when you answered questions or reviewed the material

DON'T become depressed about these areas; instead do something about them.

- Build up your knowledge by **quick tests** such as the quick quizzes in your BPP Study Text.

- Work carefully through **numerical examples** and **questions** in the Text, and refer back to the Text if you struggle with computations in the Kit.

- **Note down weaknesses** that your answers to questions contained; you are less likely to make the same mistakes if you highlight where you went wrong.

> **Breadth of revision**

Make sure your revision has sufficient **breadth**. You need to be able to answer both the compulsory questions and enough optional questions on the paper.

> **Paper 2.3**

The key to passing this paper is to spend your time practising as many questions as possible. 40 of the 55 marks in Section A will cover computational techniques so you must make a good attempt at these to pass the paper.

How to revise

There are four main ways that you can revise a topic area.

> **Write it!**
> **Read it!**
> **Teach it!**
> **Do it!**

> **Write it!**

The Course Notes and the Study Text are too bulky for revision. You need a slimmed down set of notes that summarise the key points. Writing important points down will help you recall them, particularly if your notes are presented in a way that makes it easy for you to remember them.

Read it!

You should read your notes or BPP Passcards actively, testing yourself by doing quick quizzes or writing summaries of what you have just read.

Teach it!

Exams require you to show your understanding. Teaching what you are revising to another person helps you practise explaining topics. Teaching someone who will challenge your understanding, someone for example who will be taking the same exam as you, can help both of you.

Do it!

Remember that you are revising in order to be able to answer questions in the exam. Answering questions will help you practise **technique** and **discipline**, which examiners emphasise over and over again can be crucial in passing or failing exams.

1   Start by attempting any **preparation questions** included for a particular syllabus area. These provide you with a firm foundation from which to attempt exam-standard questions.

2   The more exam-standard questions you do, the more likely you are to pass the exam. At the very least, you should attempt the **key questions** that are highlighted.

3   You should produce **full answers** under **timed conditions,** and don't cheat by looking at the answer! Look back at your notes or at your BPP Study Text instead if you are really struggling. Produce answer plans if you are running short of time.

4   Always read the **Pass marks** in the answers. They are there to help you, and will show you which points in the answer are the most important.

5   **Don't get despondent** if you didn't do very well. Refer to the **topic index** and try another question that covers the same subject.

6   When you think you can successfully answer questions on the whole syllabus, attempt the **two mock exams** at the end of the Kit. You will get the most benefit by sitting them under strict exam conditions, so that you gain experience of the four vital exam processes.

- Selecting questions
- Deciding on the order in which to attempt them
- Managing your time
- Producing answers

BPP's *Learning to Learn Accountancy* book gives further invaluable advice on how to approach revision.

BPP has also produced other vital revision aids.

- **Passcards** – Provide you with clear topic summaries and exam tips
- **Success tapes** – Help you revise on the move
- **Videos** – Show you an overview of key topics and how they are related
- **i-Pass CDs** – Offer you tests of knowledge to be completed against the clock

You can purchase these products by completing the order form at the back of this Kit or by visiting www.bpp.com/acca.

Topic	2003 Passcard chapter	Questions in this kit	Comments	Done ✓
Revision period 6 *Overseas aspects (corporate)*				
Preparation question	8	16	Useful question. Work through the answer if time is short.	
Key questions	8	17, 18	Useful questions. Answer them in full.	
Revision period 7 *Self assessment for companies*				
Key question	9	23	If you are very short of time you could prepare an answer plan for this question. However, note that this is a topical subject at the moment so don't ignore it.	
Revision period 8 *VAT*				
Preparation question	10, 11	24	Work through this answer quickly if time is short.	
Key questions	10, 11	25, 42	Useful questions. Answer in full. Question 3 of your paper will be a VAT question so it is worth being prepared for it.	
Revision period 9 *Income tax computations*				
Preparation questions	12, 16	34, 35	These are particularly important preparation questions as stakeholder pensions are very topical at the moment.	
Key questions	12, 16	36, 37	Vitally important key questions. These are the types of income tax computation that will appear in Section A. Don't forget the time apportionment of benefits	

Topic	2003 Passcard chapter	Questions in this kit	Comments	Done ✓
Revision period 10 *Employees*				
Preparation question: benefits in kind	20	43	Useful question. Work through the answer if short of time.	
Key questions	19, 20, 21	44, 45, 46	Useful questions. Answer in full. The computation of taxable benefits is frequently examined.	
Revision period 11 *Self-assessment for individuals/partnerships*				
Key questions	18	26, 27	Useful questions. Answer in full. You must practice answering written questions like this concisely. If you ramble through your answer you will overrun on time and the marker may find it hard to mark.	
Revision periods 12/13 *Schedule DI and trading losses for individuals*				
Key question: adjustment of profits	13	28	Key question that also includes basis period rules for an individual. Answer in full.	
Key question: basis periods	13	38	Useful key question on Schedule D Case I basis periods. Also income tax computation where individual dies part way through a year.	
Key questions: income tax losses	14	29, 30	Useful key questions. Answer in full. The examiner considers losses to be a core topic. They may be examined in Section A or in Question 7 of Section B.	

Topic	2003 Passcard chapter	Questions in this kit	Comments	Done ✓
Revision period 14				
Partnerships/Capital gains for individuals				
Preparation question: partnerships	15	31	This question is similar to the key question below so work through the answer if time is short. Note that you must allocate profits to each partner *before* working out what is assessed in each tax year.	
Key questions: partnerships	15	32, 33	Useful questions. Answer in full. These are standard partnership questions.	
Preparation question: capital gains	17	39	Useful question. Remember that taper relief applies to individuals only.	
Key questions: capital gains	17	40, 41	Useful questions. Answer in full.	
Revision period 15/16				
Tax planning				
Alternative Employments	22	47	Key question. Answer in full.	
Incorporation	22	48	Key question. Answer in full.	
Purchasing business	22	49	Key question. Answer in full.	
Dividends or salary	22	50	Key question. Answer in full.	

BUSINESS TAX: THE 2003 EXAMS

The examination is a **three hour paper** divided into **two sections**.

FORMAT OF THE 2003 EXAMS

	Marks
Section A: 2 compulsory questions	55
Section B: 3 (out of 5) optional 15 mark questions	45
	100

Time allowed: 3 hours

Tax rates, allowances and benefits will be given in the examination paper.

Only core topics will be examined in Section A. A non-core topic may form part of a question (such as a chargeable gain in a corporation tax computation), but this will account for a maximum of ten marks. At least 40 of the 55 available marks in Section A will be of a computational nature.

- Question 1 will be on a corporate business (for approximately 30 marks).

- Question 2 will be on an unincorporated business and/or employees (for approximately 25 marks).

The questions in Section B will be a mix of computational and written, and include the minimisation or deferment of tax liability by the identification and application of relevant exemptions and reliefs.

- Question 3 will be on VAT (either for an incorporated business or an unincorporated business).

- Question 4 will be on capital gains (either for an incorporated business or an unincorporated business).

- Question 5 will be on either groups or companies or overseas aspects.

- Question 6 will be on one of the six listed tax planning topics.

- Question 7 will be on any area of the syllabus, but will typically deal with a core topic that has not been covered in Section A. For example, partnerships, relief for trading losses or self-assessment.

Analysis of past papers

December 2002 exam

Section A

1   Adjustment of Schedule D Case I profits. Corporation tax computations. Corporation tax self assessment
2   Computation of assessable Schedule DII profits. Income tax computation. Keeping records

Section B

3   VAT: Registration, errors, deregistration
4   Computation of chargeable gains and capital gains tax liability
5   Capital gains groups
6   Employed/self employment
7   Corporation tax losses

June 2002 exam

Section A

1   Corporation tax losses
2   Calculation of Schedule D Case I adjusted profit, income tax and Class 4 NICs

Section B

3   VAT: Calculation, penalties and cash accounting scheme
4   Capital gains: reliefs
5   Overseas aspects of corporation tax
6   Alternative employments contracts
7   Partnerships

Examiner's comments

It was an excellent performance at this diet, as evidenced by the high pass rate. It was apparent candidates were very well prepared, and had obviously read the examiner's articles published in Student Accountant. Of the seven questions on the paper, only question four on capital gains was badly answered.

December 2001 exam

Section A

1   CT61. Calculation of adjusted schedule D Case I profit. Computation corporation tax.
2   Income tax losses

Section B

3   VAT: registration, pre registration input VAT, invoices, tax points
4   Capital gains: rollover relief
5   Groups of companies
6   Trading as a sole trader followed by incorporation
7   Income tax self assessment

Examiner's comments

It was pleasing to see a very good performance at this first diet of the new syllabus, and it was apparent that many candidates were very well prepared. Most candidates had obviously read my articles in Student Accountant. However, a number of candidates would have benefited by taking a bit more time reading the questions and requirements.

Pilot Paper

Section A

1   Calculation of CT payable. Quarterly payments of CT
2   IT for employee/sole trader. Payment of IT

Section B

3   VAT registration. Input tax. Deregistrations
4   Business asset taper relief. Gains on shares
5   Group relief. CT liability
6   Employee/self employed distinction. NICs. IT under Sch D II or Sch E
7   Partnership profit allocation. Losses

BPP MEETS THE EXAMINER

The examiner has provided the following answers to questions that BPP raised on the 2003 exams:

To what extent does quarterly accounting and form CT61 remain examinable?

The quarterly basis by which income tax is accounted for using Form CT61 will not be examinable from the June 2002 sitting onwards.

From June 2002 you should assume that any figures for patent royalties paid/received by a company are gross.

To what extent are charges on income examinable?

The only type of charge still examinable is a gift aid donation.

Is double tax relief examinable?

Yes but the following are **not** examinable:

(a)   The restriction on the set off of underlying tax relief
(b)   The carry back/forward of unrelieved foreign tax

Is the exemption for disposals of substantial shrareholdings examinable?

No.

How will quarterly instalments of corporation tax be examined?

Any question involving quarterly instalment payments will assume 100% of CT is paid in instalments.

Is the children's tax credit examinable?

No.

Is averaging of profits for authors and creative artists examinable?

No.

To what extent is the personal pension regime examinable?

The personal pension rules that applied until 5 April 2001 are not examinable.

Certain occupational pension schemes can apply to be subject to the new personal pension scheme rules, however, this will not be examinable.

The new rules from 6 April 2001 are examinable. The £3,600 limit for making contributions without evidence of earnings will be given in the tax rates and allowance tables. The non-tax advantages of stakeholder schemes are not examinable.

EXAM TECHNIQUE

Passing professional examinations is half about having the knowledge, and half about doing yourself full justice in the examination. You must have the right approach at the following times.

> **Before the exam**
> **Your time in the exam hall**

Before the exam

1   Set at least one **alarm** (or get an alarm call) for a morning exam.

2   Have **something to eat** but beware of eating too much; you may feel sleepy if your system is digesting a large meal.

3   Allow plenty of **time to get to the exam hall**; have your route worked out in advance and listen to news bulletins to check for potential travel problems.

4   **Don't forget** pens, pencils, rulers, erasers, watch. Also make sure you remember **entrance documentation** and **evidence of identity**.

5   Put **new batteries** into your calculator and take a spare set (or a spare calculator).

6   **Avoid discussion** about the exam with other candidates outside the exam hall.

Your time in the exam hall

1   *Read the instructions (the 'rubric') on the front of the exam paper carefully*

Check that the exam format hasn't changed. Examiners' reports often remark on the number of students who attempt too few - or too many - questions, or who attempt the wrong number of questions from different parts of the paper.

2   *Select questions carefully*

Read through the paper once, underlining the key words in the question and jotting down the most important points.   Select the optional questions that you feel you can answer best. You should base your selection on:

- The **topics** covered
- The **requirements of the whole question**
- How easy it will be to **apply the requirements** to the details you are given
- The availability of **easy marks**

Make sure that you are planning to answer the **right number of questions,** all the compulsory questions plus the correct number of optional questions.

3   *Plan your attack carefully*

Consider the **order** in which you are going to tackle questions. It is a good idea to start with your best question to boost your morale and get some easy marks 'in the bag'.

4   *Check the time allocation for each question*

Each mark carries with it a **time allocation** of 1.8 minutes (including time for selecting and reading questions, and checking answers). A 25 mark question therefore should be selected, completed and checked in 45 minutes. When time is up, you **must** go on to the next question or part. Going even one minute over the time allowed brings you a lot closer to failure.

5 *Read the question carefully and plan your answer*

Read through the question again very carefully when you come to answer it. Plan your answer taking into account how the answer should be **structured**, what the **format** should be and **how long** it should take.

Confirm before you start writing that your plan makes **sense**, covers **all relevant points** and does not include **irrelevant material.** Two minutes of planning plus eight minutes of writing is virtually certain to earn you more marks than ten minutes of writing.

6 *Answer the question set*

Particularly with written answers, make sure you **answer the question set**, and not the question you would have preferred to have been set.

7 *Gain the easy marks*

Include the obvious if it answers the question and don't try to produce the perfect answer.

Don't get bogged down in small parts of questions. If you find a part of a question difficult, get on with the rest of the question. If you are having problems with something, the chances are that everyone else is too.

8 *Produce an answer in the correct format*

The examiner will **state in the requirements** the format in which the question should be answered, for example in a report or memorandum.

9 *Follow the examiner's instructions*

You will **annoy** the examiner if you ignore him or her.

10 *Lay out your numerical computations and use workings correctly*

Make sure the layout fits the **type of question** and is in a style the examiner likes. Show all your **workings** clearly and explain what they mean. **Cross reference** them to your solution. This will help the examiner to follow your method (this is of particular importance where there may be several possible answers).

11 *Present a tidy paper*

You are a professional, and it should show in the **presentation of your work**. Students are penalised for poor presentation and so you should make sure that you write legibly, label diagrams clearly and lay out your work neatly. Markers of scripts each have hundreds of papers to mark; a badly written scrawl is unlikely to receive the same attention as a neat and well laid out paper.

12 *Stay until the end of the exam*

Use any spare time **checking and rechecking** your script. This includes checking:

- You have **filled out** the **candidate details correctly.**
- Question parts and workings are **labelled clearly.**
- Aids to navigation such as **headers and underlining** are used effectively.
- **Spelling, grammar** and **arithmetic** are correct.

13 *Don't discuss an exam with other candidates afterwards*

There's nothing more you can do about it so why discuss it?

14 ***Don't worry if you feel you have performed badly in the exam***

It is more than likely that the other candidates will have found the exam difficult too. Don't forget that there is a competitive element in these exams. As soon as you get up to leave the exam hall, *forget* **that exam** and think about the next - or, if it is the last one, celebrate!

BPP's *Learning to Learn Accountancy* book gives further invaluable advice on how to approach the day of the exam.

USEFUL WEBSITES

The websites below provide additional sources of information of relevance to your studies for *Business Taxation.*

- ACCA   www.accaglobal.com

- BPP   www.bpp.com

In particular, you should regularly check the ACCA's website to see if any articles relevant to Paper 2.3 have been published. It is essential that you read any such articles.

There was a Finance Act 2002 article in the September 2002 edition of *Student Accountant.*

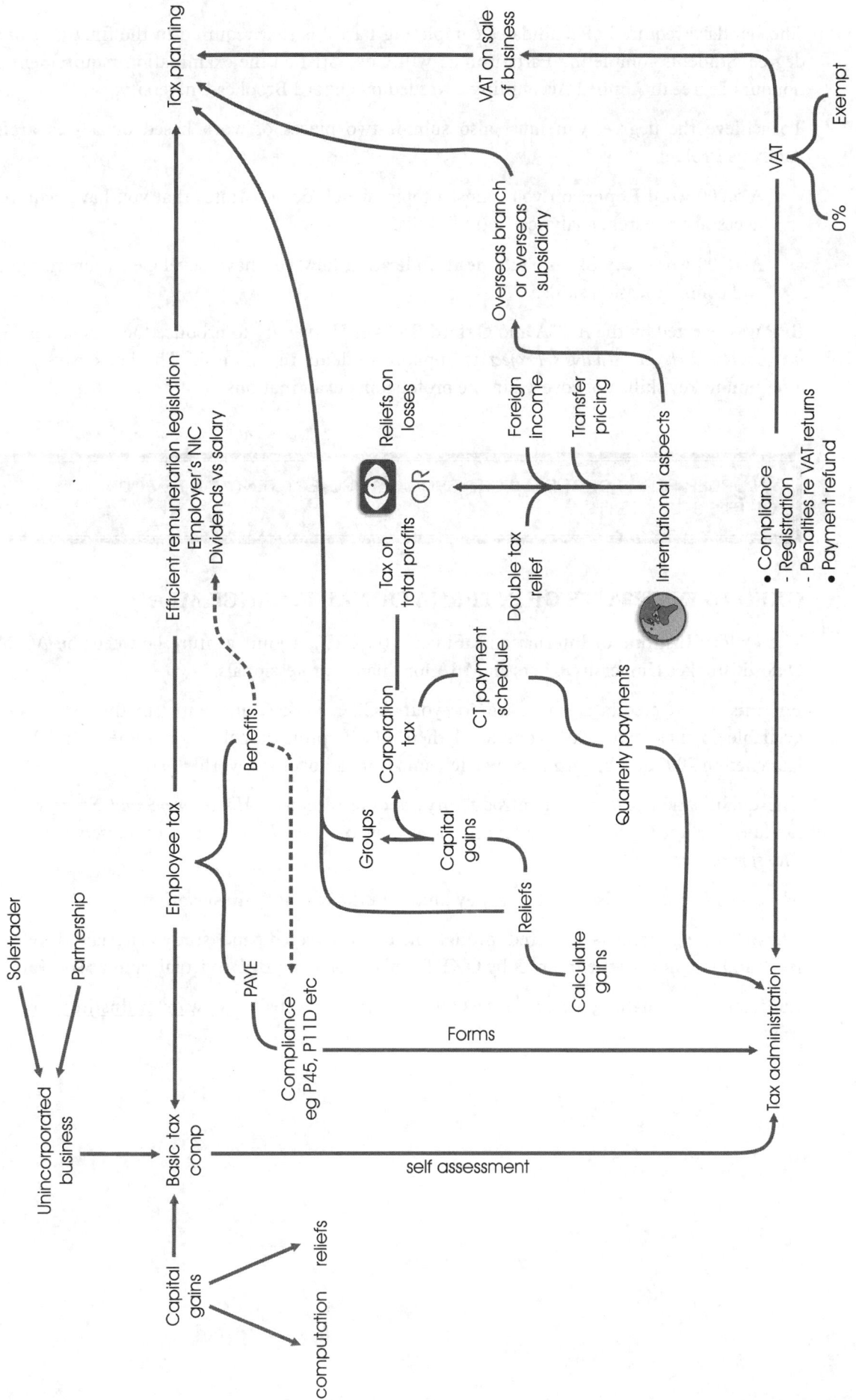

Tax planning

Soletrader

Partnership

Unincorporated business

Capital gains
- computation
- reliefs

Basic tax comp

Employee tax

Efficient remuneration legislation
Employer's NIC
Dividends vs salary

Benefits

PAYE

Compliance
eg P45, P11D etc

Groups

Capital gains

Corporation tax

CT payment schedule

Reliefs

Calculate gains

Quarterly payments

Tax on total profits

OR

Reliefs on losses

Double tax relief

Foreign income

Transfer pricing

International aspects

Overseas branch or overseas subsidiary

VAT on sale of business

VAT
- 0%
- Exempt

- Compliance
  - Registration
  - Penalties re VAT returns
- Payment refund

Forms

self assessment

Tax administration

OXFORD BROOKES BSc IN APPLIED ACCOUNTING

The standard required of candidates completing Part 2 is that required in the final year of a UK degree. Students completing Parts 1 and 2 will have satisfied the examination requirement for an honours degree in Applied Accounting, awarded by Oxford Brookes University.

To achieve the degree, you must also submit two pieces of work based on a **Research and Analysis Project.**

- A 5,000 word **Report** on your chosen topic, which demonstrates that you have acquired the necessary research, analytical and IT skills.

- A 1,500 word **Key Skills Statement**, indicating how you have developed your interpersonal and communication skills.

BPP was selected by the ACCA and Oxford Brookes University to produce the official text *Success in your Research and Analysis Project* to support students in this task. The book pays particular attention to key skills not covered in the professional examinations.

AN ORDER FORM FOR THE OXFORD BROOKES PROJECT TEXT CAN BE FOUND AT THE END OF THIS STUDY TEXT.

OXFORD INSTITUTE OF INTERNATIONAL FINANCE MBA

The Oxford Institute of International Finance (OXIIF), a joint venture between the ACCA and Oxford Brookes University, offers an MBA for finance professionals.

For this MBA, credits are awarded for your ACCA studies, and entry to the MBA course is available to those who have completed their ACCA professional stage studies. The MBA was launched in 2002 and has attracted participants from all over the world.

The qualification features an introductory module (*Markets, Management and Strategy*). Other modules include *Global Business Strategy, Managing Self Development,* and *Organisational Change & Transformation.*

Research Methods are also taught, as they underpin the **research dissertation**.

The MBA programme is delivered through the use of targeted paper study materials, developed by BPP, and taught over the Internet by OXIIF personnel using BPP's virtual campus software.

For further information, please see the Oxford Institute's website: www.oxfordinstitute.org.

Questions

CORPORATE BUSINESSES

Questions 1 to 25 cover corporate businesses, the subject of Part A of the BPP Study Text for Paper 2.3.

1   PREPARATION QUESTION: SUNDRY ADJUSTMENTS

Advise the management of a limited company as to the consequences for corporation tax purposes of the following transactions which have occurred during its last accounting period.

(a)   Loan interest of £5,000 was received. The borrower (a UK company) advised that no tax had been deducted from the interest. The loan was a non-trading investment.

(b)   £100,000 was received from the sale of a factory in respect of which capital allowances had been claimed. The factory was purchased new and first used in 1988. It had always been used as a factory.

(c)   Defalcations of cash by staff have been discovered in the sum of £8,000, of which £5,000 was attributable to junior staff and the balance to a member of the board of directors.

(d)   Additional retail premises were acquired for £40,000, which was well below normal market value due to the dilapidated state of these premises. Repairs and renewals expenditure of £60,000 had to be incurred.

(e)   Expenditure totalling £128,000 was incurred in entertaining the company's own staff, customers' staff and representatives from both UK and foreign business agencies.

Guidance notes

1   You can deal with each item separately, not worrying about the other items. The important thing is to state the treatment of each item clearly.

2   Capital allowances are not the only tax aspect of the sale of the factory to consider.

3   With the defalcations, the position of the guilty party is relevant. Directors run the business, and are therefore treated differently from junior staff.

4   With the retail premises, there is a legal case of particular relevance.

5   When entertaining expenditure is incurred, the tax treatment depends on who was entertained.

2   PREPARATION QUESTION: CAPITAL AND REVENUE

In taxation, the distinction between capital and revenue expenditure is crucial.

Required

Indicate how this distinction is applied when dealing with items appearing in a company's profit and loss account, supporting your answer by reference to relevant case law.

Guidance notes

1   Start by outlining the distinction. Why does it matter if expenditure is capital or if a profit is a capital gain?

2   Then explain what expenditure is likely to be treated as capital, giving some examples. A good area is repairs and improvements.

3   Cite cases by name if you can, but always make sure you outline the facts and show clearly why the case is relevant.

4   Finally, consider what makes a profit a capital gain.

3   TRUNK LTD

27 mins

The profit and loss account of Trunk Ltd, a manufacturing company, for the year ended 31 March 2003 showed a loss of £42,000 after accounting for the under-noted items.

Note	Expenditure	£	£	Income	£
(1)	Premium on lease		2,000		
	Depreciation		9,500	Discount received	3,200
	Patent fees (not royalties)		4,000	Insurance recovery re flood	
	Debenture interest (gross:			damage to stock	6,500
	trading relationship)		8,000	Rents received	10,000
	Loss on sale of lorry		6,000	Gain on sale of plant	7,400
	Bad debts:				
	Amounts written off	4,000			
	Increase special provision	2,000			
		6,000			
	Less:				
	Reduction general provision	1,000			
			5,000		

Note	Expenditure	£
(2)	Entertainment expenses	2,600
	Legal fees:	
	Re new lease	3,200
	Re recovery of loan to former employee	1,200
	Re employees' service contracts	600
(3)	General expenses	4,000
(4)	Repairs and renewals	6,400

Capital allowances for the accounting period were agreed at £7,160.

Notes

(1) This represents the amount written off in respect of a premium of £20,000 paid by the company on being granted a ten-year lease on its premises on 1 April 2002.

(2) Entertainment consists of expenditure on:

	£
Entertaining customers	1,200
Staff dance (40 people)	800
Gifts to customers of food hampers	600

(3) General expenses comprise:

	£
Penalty for late VAT return	2,200
Parking fines on company cars	300
Fees for employees attending courses	1,500

(4) Included in this figure for repairs is an amount of £5,000 incurred in installing new windows in a recently-acquired second-hand warehouse. This building had suffered fire damage resulting in all of its windows being blown out shortly before being acquired by Trunk Ltd. Other repairs were of a routine nature.

Required

Compute the adjusted Schedule D Case I figure for the above period.

Your answer should show clearly your reasons for your treatment of each of the above items including those items not included in your computation.   **(15 marks)**

4 SCHEDULE D ADJUSTMENTS

27 mins

An examination of the draft accounts of your company for the year ended 31 March 2003 reveals the following details in respect of specific items of expenditure and income. The draft accounts showed a profit of £290,000.

EXPENDITURE

(a) Throughout the year, two of the directors were seconded to work elsewhere. One worked for Oxfam - a leading charity - and his salary, paid by your company, was £22,000. The other worked for a subsidiary company in the group and his salary, also paid by your company, was £24,000.

(b) Damages of £30,000 were paid to a customer who was injured by a falling crate while visiting your factory. Only £18,000 was recovered from your public liability insurers.

(c) During the year the company purchased freehold offices for £40,000. Your chief engineer estimated that it would cost £2,000 to get them ready for use. In the event it cost £12,000. The amount spent purchasing the offices was capitalised but the repair expenditure of £12,000 was deducted in the profit and loss account.

(d) Bad debts were written off amounting to £6,000. The appropriate ledger account for the year showed:

	£		£
Trade debts written off	8,000	Balances b/fwd:	
Employee loans written off	2,000	Special provision	10,000
Balances c/fwd:		General provisions	8,000
Special provision	12,000	Bad debts recovered	3,000
General provision	5,000	Profit and loss account	6,000
	27,000		27,000

(e) Because of an overall contraction in trade, a supervisor was made redundant and given a severance payment of £18,000. His statutory redundancy entitlement was £11,000.

INCOME

(f) During the year the company obtained recoveries from its insurers amounting to £32,000. These related to damage caused and repairs completed in the year to 31 March 2002 and comprised:

	£
In respect of repairs to the general office	18,000
In respect of repairs to property let by the company to another firm	14,000
	32,000

(g) Goods were sold to a subsidiary in the Caribbean for £80,000. Had they been sold to a UK customer the price would have been £120,000.

Required

Compute the adjusted Schedule D Case I profit starting with the profit of £290,000 shown by the accounts. Give reasons for your adjustments, quoting case law where appropriate.

(15 marks)

5 PREPARATION QUESTION: CORPORATION TAX COMPUTATION

Abel Ltd, a UK trading company, produced the following results for the year ended 31 March 2003.

	£
Income	
Adjusted trading profit	245,000
Rental income	15,000
Bank deposit interest accrued (non-trading investment)	4,000
Capital gains: 25 September 2002	35,000
28 March 2003	7,000
(There were capital losses of £8,000 brought forward at 1 April 2002.)	
Dividends from UK companies (including tax credits)	15,000
Charges paid	
Gift aid donation	7,000

Required

(a) Compute the mainstream corporation tax (MCT) payable by Abel Ltd for the above accounting period.

(b) Advise the directors of the effect on the company's tax liability of their decision to make the asset sale on 28 March 2003.

Guidance notes

1   In working out a company's profits chargeable to corporation tax (PCTCT), we must bring together all taxable profits, including gains. You must therefore start by drawing up a working, and picking out from the question all relevant profit figures.

2   Once you have found the PCTCT, you can consider the rate of tax. You should find that small companies marginal relief applies. If you do not, look carefully to see whether you have missed anything.

3   Having completed your computation, you should move on to part (b). The answer will become clear if you remember that everyone would like to pay less tax, and to pay their tax later.

6 PREPARATION QUESTION: LONG PERIOD OF ACCOUNT

Hartlington Ltd is a UK resident company. It was incorporated in 1998 and began its trade of manufacturing paper-making machinery in the same year. The company's recent results are as follows.

	Year ended 31 March 2001 £	Period 1 April 2001 to 30 Sept 2002 £
Trading profits (as adjusted for taxation but before capital allowances)	148,000	477,900
Bank interest accrued (non-trading investment)	18,000	20,500
Chargeable gains on sales of shares	108,000	176,250
Dividends received (net) from UK companies	788	9,205
Gift aid donations paid	3,750	5,250

Other relevant information is as follows.

(a) *Plant and machinery*

The balance in the pool at 1 April 2000 was £213,000. Purchases and sales of assets qualifying for capital allowances were as follows.

Year ended 31 March 2001

Purchases

31.1.01	Six cars for sales staff at a cost of £6,000 each
31.3.01	Car for the managing director £16,500

Period 1 April 2001 to 30 September 2002

Purchases

6.5.01	Plant and machinery £119,583
30.9.01	Car for the chief accountant £7,800
7.6.02	New computer equipment £23,000

Sales

30.11.01	Plant and machinery £70,000 (cost £150,000 in 1998)
1.6.02	Two cars at a price of £1,997 each (both were purchased in 1998 for £4,500 each)

None of the expenditure is to be treated as incurred on either short-life assets or on long-life assets. The business is a small enterprise for FYA purposes.

(b)   Payments and receipts in the period from 1 April 2001 to 30 September 2002 were as follows.

		£
(i)	Bank interest received	
	30.9.01	5,250
	31.3.02	9,791
	30.9.02	5,459

All interest was received at the end of the six month period for which it accrued.

(ii)	Chargeable gains	
	30.6.02	176,250
(iii)	Dividends received (net)	
	30.9.01	1,000
	31.3.02	598
	30.9.02	7,785
(iv)	Gift aid donations paid	
	30.6.01	3,750
	30.6.02	1,500

Required

Calculate the corporation tax payable for the periods in the question and state the due dates of payment.

Guidance notes

1   You are asked to calculate the corporation tax payable for three accounting periods. The simplest (and quickest) way to do this is to set up three columns.

2   Set out the computation in the normal way, beginning with trading profits, followed by capital allowances, investment income, gains and charges.

3   The resulting figure is profits chargeable to corporation tax (PCTCT). Remember that dividends plus tax credits are added to PCTCT to calculate 'profits'. Dividends are grossed up by multiplying by $^{100}/_{90}$.

4   Calculating the tax payable involves a number of steps, which should be taken in the right order.

   (a)   Decide which financial year(s) the accounting period falls into, so that the appropriate tax rates and upper and lower limits are used.

   (b)   Calculate the corporation tax.

(c)   If relevant, calculate and deduct marginal relief, remembering to adjust the limits for periods of less than 12 months.

5   Don't overlook the easy mark available for stating the due date for payment of the tax in each period.

7   UNUSUAL URNS LTD   *52 mins*

(a)   Unusual Urns Limited (UUL) is a United Kingdom resident company which manufactures pottery. It has no associated companies.

The company's results for the year ended 31 January 2003 were as follows.

	£
Trading profits (as adjusted for taxation but before capital allowances)	900,000
Income	
Bank interest (note 2)	5,000
Loan interest (note 3)	40,000
Expenditure	
Gift aid donation (note 4)	20,000

Notes

1   UUL is a medium-sized company with a turnover in the year ended 31 January 2003 of £8,000,000. The average number of employees during the accounting period was 120.

2   *Bank interest*

		£
31.7.02	Received	2,000
31.1.03	Received	3,000
		5,000

The interest was non-trading income. There were no accrued amounts at the beginning or end of the year.

3   *Loan interest*

		£
31.7.02	Received	20,000
31.1.03	Received	20,000
		40,000

(a)   The interest was received gross from another UK company

(b)   The interest was non-trading income

(c)   The loan was made on 1.4.02

(d)   There were no accrued amounts at the end of the year.

4   *Gift aid donation*

The gift aid donation was paid on 1 July 2002.

5   *Plant and machinery*

On 1 February 2002 the tax written down values of plant and machinery were as follows.

	£
Pool	223,000
'Short-life' asset	2,500
Expensive car (1)	16,000

During the year ended 31 January 2003 the following capital transactions took place.

Purchases

		£
1.4.02	Machinery	280,000
1.8.02	Expensive car (2)	35,000
1.9.02	Machinery	45,000
1.10.02	Cars (not 'expensive')	60,000
1.12.02	Lorry	55,000

Sales

		£
1.5.02	Machinery	40,000
1.8.02	Expensive car (1)	18,000
1.10.02	Cars (not 'expensive')	20,000
1.11.02	Short-life asset (purchased 31.12.00)	500

Notes

(1)   The two purchases of machinery and the lorry are not to be treated as either 'short-life' assets or 'long-life' assets.

(2)   No asset was sold for an amount greater than cost.

(3)   None of the machinery acquired was computer or information technology equipment.

6   *Industrial buildings*

During 1998 UUL had erected a factory which was brought into use in December 1998. The costs incurred were as follows.

	£
Land	60,000
Legal expenses on acquisition of land	3,000
Levelling land	2,000
Factory	100,000
Architect's fees on construction of factory	6,000

Included in the costs of the factory were administrative offices (£10,000) and a design office (£5,000).

In August/September 2002 the administration offices were extended at a cost of £30,000.

Required

Calculate the corporation tax payable for the year ended 31 January 2003 and state the due date for the payment of the tax.   (22 marks)

(b)   The results of Unusual Urns Limited for the previous two accounting periods were as follows.

	Year ended 31.7.01 £	6 months to 31.1.02 £
Schedule D		
Case I profit/(loss)	210,000	(150,000)
Charges on income:		
Gift aid donations	7,500	10,000

Required

(i)   State the alternative methods by which UUL can obtain relief for the loss of £150,000 sustained in the period ended 31 January 2002; and

(ii)   State, with your reasons, which of the alternative loss utilisation methods you have described in (b)(i) above you would choose to obtain the maximum tax advantage when claiming loss relief in respect of the £150,000 loss. You should also state what effect your proposed treatment of the losses will have on the charges on income paid.   (7 marks)

(29 marks)

Notes

1   Calculations are not required in part (b).

2   None of the information provided in part (b) of the question is to be taken into account when answering part (a) of the question.

8   UNFORSEEN ULTRASONICS LIMITED   *50 mins*

Unforeseen Ultrasonics Limited (UUL) is a United Kingdom resident company which manufactures accessories for telecommunication systems. It has no associated companies.

The company's results for the year ended 31 December 2002 were as follows.

	£
Trading profits (adjusted for taxation but before capital allowances) (note 1)	2,300,000
Bank interest receivable (non-trading investment)	1,500
Debenture interest received (non-trading investment) (note 4)	80,000
Payment under the gift aid scheme to a national charity (paid September 2002)	5,000

The company has traded in a purpose built unit since 1 January 1998. The total cost of the unit was made up as follows:

	£
Freehold land	50,000
Manufacturing area	240,000
Canteen	30,000
Design office *-Drawing*	90,000
General office *<25%?*	70,000
	480,000

Take into account.

On 1 July 2002 an extension to the general office was completed costing £60,000.

On 1 January 2002 the tax written-down values of plant and machinery were as follows.

	£
Pool	190,000
Short-life asset	4,000

Allowed up to 4 Years.

The short-life asset was purchased on 1 December 1997 and was sold on 31 July 2002 for £10,000.

On 1 August 2002 a new car costing £18,000 was purchased for the managing director. The car previously used by him had cost £10,000 in April 2000 and was sold for £8,000. A new precision engineering machine was purchased on 1 August 2002 for £56,250.

On 1 September 2002, Unforeseen Ultrasonics Limited sold a piece of land for £72,493. The land had been acquired as an investment in July 1988 for £27,000. *√ Capital gain.*

Notes

1   In arriving at the adjusted trading profit an adjustment had been made for small capital additions totalling £24,375 which the company had written off as repairs but which the Inspector of Taxes had insisted were added back.

2   On 1 January 2002 the company had capital losses brought forward of £30,000. *– against Capital gain.*

3   On 1 January 2002 the company had trading losses brought forward of £600,000.

4   The debenture was invested in on 1 April 2002. All amounts accrued in the nine months to 31.12.02 were received in the period.

5   The company paid corporation tax at the full rate in its accounting period ended 31 December 2001. *– was large company previous year.*

6   The company is a small or medium sized enterprise for capital allowance purposes.

Required

Calculate the mainstream corporation tax payable for the year ended 31 December 2002 and state the due date(s) for payment of this amount and the amount of any losses carried forward.   **(28 marks)**

Assume indexation factor July 1988 – September 2002 0.642

9   INDUSTRIAL LTD (PILOT PAPER)   *54 mins*

Industrial Ltd is a UK resident company that manufactures furniture. The company's results for the year ended 31 March 2003 are summarised as follows:

	£
Trading profit (as adjusted for taxation but before taking account of capital allowances and patent royalties)	1,689,710
Income from property (note 1)	110,400
Bank interest received (note 2)	12,500
Loan interest received (note 3)	36,000
Profit on disposal of shares (note 4)	87,200
Patent royalties payable (note 5)	(12,000)
Donation to charity (note 6)	(1,500)

Note 1 – Income from property

Since 1 January 2003 Industrial Ltd has leased an office building that is surplus to requirements. On that date the company received a premium of £80,000 for the grant of a ten-year lease, and the annual rent of £30,400 which is payable in advance.

Note 2 – Bank interest received

The bank interest was received on 31 March 2003. The bank deposits are held for non-trading purposes. There were no accruals of bank interest at the beginning or end of the year.

Note 3 – Loan interest received

The loan interest was received on 31 March 2003. The loan was made for non-trading purposes to another UK company. There were no accruals of loan interest at the beginning or end of the year.

Note 4 – Profit on disposal of shares

The profit on disposal of shares is in respect of a shareholding that was sold on 15 January 2003 for £223,000. The shareholding was purchased on 1 April 1999 for £135,800. The indexation allowance from April 1999 to January 2003 is £8,827.

At 1 April 2002 Industrial Ltd had unused capital losses brought forward of £10,800.

Note 5 – Patent royalties payable

The figure for patent royalties payable is calculated as follows:

	£
Payments made	11,500
Accrued at 31 March 2003	2,000
	13,500
Accrued at 1 April 2002	(1,500)
	12,000

All patent royalties were paid to other UK companies. The amount of patent royalties charged in the accounts was the amount accrued in the year.

Note 6 – Donation to charity

The donation to charity was the amount paid under the Gift Aid Scheme.

Note 7 – Industrial building

Industrial Ltd has a new factory constructed at a cost of £400,000 that was brought into use on 30 September 2002.

	£
Land	80,000
Levelling the land	9,200
Architects fees	24,300
Heating system	12,800
Fire alarm system	7,200
Strengthened concrete floor to support machinery	16,500
General offices	62,500
Factory	187,500
	400,000

Note 8 – Plant and machinery

On 1 April 2002 the tax written down values of plant and machinery were as follows:

	£
General pool	84,600
Expensive motor car	15,400

The expensive motor car was sold on 31 August 2002 for £19,600.

In addition to any items of plant and machinery included in the cost of the industrial building (see note 7), the following assets were purchased during the year ended 31 March 2003.

		£
15 June 2002	Computer	3,400
15 August 2002	Motor car	17,200
12 October 2002	Lorry	32,000

Industrial Ltd is a medium-sized company as defined by the Companies Acts.

Note 9 – Other information

Industrial Ltd has no associated companies. For the year ended 31 March 2002 Industrial Ltd had profits chargeable to corporation tax of £1,650,000.

Required

(a) Calculate the corporation tax payable by Industrial Ltd for the year ended 31 March 2003.   (25 marks)

(b) (i) Explain why Industrial Ltd is required to make quarterly instalment payments in respect of its corporation tax liability for the year ended 31 March 2003.   (2 marks)

   (ii) State the relevant due dates for payment of the corporation tax liability. (3 marks)

(30 marks)

10 PREPARATION QUESTION: PLANT AND A FACTORY

Freddie Ltd prepared accounts for the ten month period to 31 March 2003.

The following capital expenditure was incurred in this trading period.

(i)   30 January 2003   New computer equipment costing £2,500.

(ii) 1 February 2003   New motor car costing £16,000, secondhand motor car costing £5,000.

(iii) 2 March 2003   New plant costing £32,400, secondhand plant costing £33,442, secondhand factory and land costing £50,000 (including land £15,000) which had been purchased new by the original owner on 5 June 1988 for £10,000 (including land £2,500), and had always been used as a factory.

(iv) 31 March 2003   Extension to the factory built for £222,000.

Prior to 1 July 2002, all equipment was leased so there were no tax written down values brought forward on this date.

Freddie Ltd's business qualifies as a small enterprise for capital allowance purposes.

Required

(a) Calculate the maximum capital allowances which can be claimed by Freddie Ltd in this accounting period.

(b) Set out the amount of tax benefit the reliefs calculated in (a) would yield and when this benefit would be obtained.

(c) Outline the relief available to Freddie Ltd in respect of expenditure on office accommodation.

Assume tax rates and allowances for FY 2002 throughout this period.

Guidance notes

1   You should first read through the question, and note all the different types of asset involved.

2   You can then plan how your answer will look. Because there is only one accounting period, there is no real need for a multi-column computation.

3   Each type of asset should then be tackled separately. By breaking the question down into small pieces in this way, it becomes much more manageable.

4   Note the length of the accounting period. Will this affect WDAs or FYAs?

11 UNFORGETTABLE UNITS LIMITED   *50 mins*

Unforgettable Units Limited (UUL) is a United Kingdom resident company which manufactures self-assemble furniture. It has no associated companies and has always made accounts up to 31 August. In the year ended 31 August 2002 the company's profit was £822,875 which was arrived at *after* charging and crediting the following items.

Expenditure		£
Gift aid donations paid		58,000
Legal expenses	(note 2)	10,000
Bad debts	(note 3)	42,000
Income		
Debenture interest	(note 4)	64,000
Bank interest	(note 5)	5,000
Dividend	(note 6)	11,250

Note 1

Unforgettable Units Limited is a medium-sized company with a turnover in the year ended 31 August 2002 of £4,000,000. The average number of employees during the accounting period was 160.

Note 2

Legal expenses incurred were:

Fine for not fitting saws with protective guards   £10,000

Note 3

Bad debts account

	£		£
Trading debts written off in year	23,000	Balances at 1.9.01	
		– Specific	57,000
Balances at 31.8.02		– General	40,000
– Specific	92,000	Recovery of bad debt previously	
– General	35,000	written off	11,000
		Profit and loss account	42,000
	150,000		150,000

Note 4

Debenture interest receivable

	£		£
1.9.01 b/f	–	30.4.02 received	61,000
Profit and loss account	64,000	31.8.02 c/f	3,000
	64,000		64,000

The interest was non-trading income.

Note 5

Bank interest

The £5,000 was credited to the company's bank account on 31 July 2002. The interest is non-trading interest.

Note 6

On 1 December 2001 Unforgettable Units Limited received a dividend from another UK company of £11,250. This amount represents the actual amount received without any adjustment for tax credits.

Note 7

Plant and machinery

On 1 September 2001 the tax written down values of plant and machinery was:

	£
Main pool	100,000

New machinery, which is not to be treated either a 'short-life' asset or a 'long-life' asset, costing £35,000 was purchased on 31 January 2002. On 1 May 2002 a car that had cost £7,500 in 2000 was sold for £2,000 and replaced with one costing £13,000.

Note 8

Industrial buildings allowance

On 1 January 2002 Unforgettable Units Limited purchased a factory for £150,000 from Cape Capsules Limited whose accounting date was 31 March. The factory was built for Cape

Capsules Limited at a cost of £250,000 and had been brought into use on 1 August 1996. Maximum industrial buildings allowances had been claimed by Cape Capsules Limited. The factory has not been used for non-trading purposes.

Required

Calculate the corporation tax payable by Unforgettable Units Limited for the year ended 31 August 2002. You should give reasons for your treatment of the legal expenses in Note 3.

(28 marks)

12   PREPARATION QUESTION: CARRYING BACK A LOSS

Galbraith Ltd is a company resident in the United Kingdom making garments for sale to the tourist industry at its factory in Callander. It started to trade on 1 April 2000. The company's results for the first three years are as follows.

| | *Year ended 31 March* | | |
	2001	2002	2003
	£	£	£
Trading profit/(loss) (as adjusted for taxation)	125,000	(465,000)	50,000
Bank interest accrued (non-trading investment)	263,000	10,000	24,000
Chargeable gains /(allowable loss)	60,360	(7,000)	3,000
Dividends received from UK companies (net) (January)	6,750	3,000	3,750
Gift aid donation	40,000	47,000	30,000

Required

(a) Calculate the corporation tax liabilities for the three years after claiming maximum loss relief at the earliest possible times. Comment on the effectiveness of the reliefs. Assume FY 2002 rates and allowances apply throughout.

(b) In respect of the mainstream corporation tax for the accounting period ended 31 March 2003, state when this will be due for payment and state the filing date.

Guidance notes

1   In requirement (a) you are alerted to the likelihood of encountering losses.

2   First, set out the figures for trading profits and leave space for losses carried forward under s 393(1) ICTA 1988.

3   Set out the remainder of the profits subject to tax and then deduct losses from the total. Questions usually require loss relief to be claimed as quickly as possible. Remember that s 393A(1) ICTA 1988 requires losses to be set off first against total profits of the loss-making accounting period. Only after these have been extinguished can losses be carried back. Any remaining losses are carried forward, but may only be set against trading profits (not total profits).

4   Remember that certain companies pay corporation tax at the starting rate of 0%. Does the starting rate of corporation tax apply in this case?

5   Remember that certain companies are required to pay for their anticipated corporation tax liability by quarterly instalments. Does this apply to Galbraith Ltd?

13   UNPLUGGED UTENSILS LTD   *27 mins*

Unplugged Utensils Limited (UUL) is a United Kingdom resident company which has been manufacturing kitchen appliances since 1993. It has no associated companies. The following is a summary of the company's results:

	Year ended 31.7.99	Year ended 31.7.00	Year ended 31.7.01	Five months to 31.12.01	Year ended 31.12.02	Year ended 31.12.03 (forecast)
	£	£	£	£	£	£
Schedule D1						
Profit/(loss)	150,000	50,000	(50,000)	58,000	(200,000)	50,000
Schedule A	4,000	-	22,000	-	20,000	-
Chargeable gains/(losses)	-	5,000	-	(6,000)	5,000	-
Bank interest received	-	-	20,000	10,000	-	4,000
Gift aid payment	-	2,000	2,000	2,000	4,000	4,000

Notes

1   The gift paid payment was the actual amount paid on 30 November each year.

2   All interest accrued in the year it was received.

3   The company had no losses to carry forward at 31 July 1998.

4   Assume tax rates and allowances remain unchanged after 1.4.02.

Required

(a)   Calculate the corporation tax liabilities for all years in the question after giving maximum relief at the earliest time for the losses sustained.   (12 marks)

(b)   Show any balances carried forward.   (3 marks)

                                                   (15 marks)

14   PREPARATION QUESTION: A BUILDING AND SHARES

Jolly Cove Ltd, which commenced trading in 1983, makes up its accounts annually to 31 March, and has no associated companies.

During its accounting year ended 31 March 2003 Jolly Cove Ltd disposed of the following assets.

(a)   In June 2002, a non-industrial building was sold for £200,000. It had been purchased in July 1984 for £65,000.

(b)   In July 2002, 4,000 shares in Z plc were sold for £22,000. The shares in Z plc had been acquired as follows.

      May 1982   2,000 shares for £4,000
      March 1986   2,000 shares for £5,000

There were no capital losses brought forward.

Jolly Cove Ltd's taxable profits for the year ended 31 March 2003, excluding capital gains, were £2,000,000.

Required

(a)   Calculate the amount of corporation tax payable as a result of the above transactions.

(b)   Advise Jolly Cove Ltd as to the consequences of its replacing the building referred to above with another building costing either £225,000 or alternatively £175,000.

Assume indexation factors:

July 1984 – June 2002	0.960
May 1982 – April 1985	0.162
April 1985 – March 1986	0.02
March 1986 – July 2002	0.808

Guidance notes

1   The building requires a basic capital gains computation.

2   The shares are in the FA 1985 pool. The FA 1985 pool includes indexation within it, firstly up to its starting point April 1985 and then up to each purchase or sale. Strictly, there is no need to round indexation post April 1985, but for exam purposes you may use the rounded factors given to you in the exam.

3   Part (b) is about rollover relief. Remember that the general rule is that someone who sells an asset and claims rollover relief will still be taxed on the gain immediately, to the extent of the cash they put into their pocket instead of into the new asset.

15   ABC LTD

27 mins

ABC Ltd, a UK resident company which manufactures concrete slabs, owns 8,000 shares in DEF Ltd, a retail company which sells building materials to the public. This holding represents 80% of the share capital of DEF Ltd.

ABC Ltd needs to raise approximately £512,000 in order to repay a loan which is due for repayment in June 2003.

The directors of the company advised you in October 2002 that they were considering the sale of two assets, each of which could be sold for £700,000. They sought your advice on which of the two assets would generate sufficient funds, after taking into account any corporation tax payable on the resultant gain, to repay the outstanding loan. It was the directors' intention to sell the appropriate asset in December 2002, during ABC Ltd's accounting period of twelve months to 31 March 2003.

Details of the two assets, only ONE of which was to be sold, are as follows;

(a)   A plot of land which had cost £130,000 in June 1996 and which is used for the storage of finished products.

This purchase had been funded by the sale in May 1995, for £140,000, of another plot of land, used for parking the company's vehicles. This land had cost £80,000 in May 1988.

On the occasion of this first sale, the maximum possible rollover relief was claimed.

(b)   The 80% holding of shares in DEF Ltd

These shares had cost £40,000 in May 1989.

Prior to the current proposed disposal, ABC Ltd had not made any other disposals since May 1995.

You establish that ABC Ltd's other chargeable income for the year ended 31 March 2003 will be £150,000.

Required

(a)   Compute the chargeable gain which will arise as a result of each of the two proposed disposals.   (10 marks)

(b)   Advise the directors of ABC Ltd which asset will generate sufficient funds, after taking into account the corporation tax payable on the gain, to allow them to repay the outstanding loan.   (5 marks)

Please note that this question does NOT require you to calculate the TOTAL corporation tax payable by ABC Ltd.   **(15 marks)**

Assume indexation factors:

May 1988 – May 1995	0.409
June 1996 – December 2002	0.149
May 1989 – December 2002	0.529

16   PREPARATION QUESTION: FOREIGN TAX

Mumbo Ltd, a UK resident trading company, owns 6% of the share capital of Z Inc and 8% of the share capital of X SA. Neither of these companies is resident in the UK for tax purposes. In addition, Mumbo Ltd has a controlling interest in four UK resident companies.

The following information relates to Mumbo Ltd's 12 month accounting period ended 30 April 2003.

	£	£
Income		
Schedule D Case I trading profits		550,000
Schedule D Case V		
Dividend from Z Inc - after deduction of withholding tax of 28%	36,000	
Dividend from X SA - after deduction of withholding tax of 5%	38,000	
		74,000
Charge paid		
Gift aid donation		60,000

Required

Compute the MCT payable for the above period by Mumbo Ltd, showing clearly the relief for double taxation. Assume FY 2002 tax rates and allowances apply throughout.

Guidance notes

1   This question requires you to compute mainstream corporation tax on overseas income, taking account of double taxation relief.

2   Charges should be set first against UK profits and then against the overseas income which has borne the lowest rate of overseas tax.

3   The restriction of double taxation relief to the lower of the overseas tax and the UK tax on the overseas income must be applied to each source of income separately.

17   B AND W LTD   *27 mins*

B Ltd acquired 80% of the voting rights of W Ltd in December 2001. Both companies are resident in the United Kingdom. B Ltd has, for several years, owned 5% of the voting capital of P Inc, a company resident abroad.

The following information relates to B Ltd for its twelve-month accounting period ended 31 January 2003.

	£
INCOME	
Adjusted trading profits	296,000
Capital gains	30,000
Dividend from P Inc (net of 20% overseas tax)	1,600
Debenture interest received 30 November 2002 (non trading investment)	8,000
FII (inclusive of tax credit) received in May 2002	32,000
CHARGES PAID	
Gift Aid to charity	18,000

W Ltd also made up accounts for the twelve months to 31 January 2003 and its only taxable income consisted of trading profits of £6,000.

There were no accruals of debenture interest at the beginning or end of the year. The debenture interest was received gross from another UK company.

Required

Compute the mainstream corporation tax (MCT) payable by both B Ltd and W Ltd for the above accounting period, assuming all appropriate claims are made.

Show clearly your treatment of double tax relief. **(15 marks)**

18 **X LTD** *27 mins*

X Ltd, a company resident in the United Kingdom, makes up accounts each year to 30 April. It acquired a 55% interest in Z Ltd on 30 November 2002 and a 60% interest in Y Ltd on 30 December 2002.

During its year ended 30 April 2003, X Ltd had an adjusted trading profit (before capital allowances) of £220,000. The company let various properties to other businesses and, during the year to 30 April 2003, this activity resulted in a loss of £17,000. *– Set against current profits after charges.*

The other income and payments during the year ended 30 April 2003 were:

INCOME

(Gross figures - including tax credits where relevant)	£
Bank interest accrued	40,000
Dividend from foreign company (withholding tax was 25%)	4,000
Franked Investment Income (FII) (received May 2002)	15,000

PAYMENTS:	£
Gift Aid payment to charity	8,000

The balances for capital allowances purposes at 1 May 2002 were:

General pool	£102,000
Expensive car	£18,000

During the year there were two items bought - plant, costing £12,000, on 30 May 2002, and a lorry, costing £23,750, on 31 July 2002.

The company is a small enterprise for first year allowance purposes.

Required

(a) Compute the capital allowances claimable for the year ended 30 April 2003. (3 marks)

(b) Compute the mainstream corporation tax (MCT) payable for the year ended 30 April 2003, showing clearly your treatment of DTR. State the due date of payment of the tax.

Assume FY 2002 tax rates and allowances continue to apply. (12 marks)

(15 marks)

19   PREPARATION QUESTION: GROUP RELIEF

P Ltd owns the following holdings in ordinary shares in other companies, which are all UK resident.

Q Ltd	83%
R Ltd	77%
S Ltd	67%
M Ltd	80%

The ordinary shares of P Ltd are owned to the extent of 62% by Mr C, who also owns 70% of the ordinary shares of T Ltd, another UK resident company. In each case, the other conditions for claiming group relief, where appropriate, are satisfied.

The following are the results of the above companies for the year ended 31 March 2003.

	M Ltd £	P Ltd £	Q Ltd £	R Ltd £	S Ltd £	T Ltd £
Income						
Trading profit	10,000	0	64,000	260,000	0	70,000
Trading loss	0	223,000	0	0	8,000	0
Schedule A	0	6,000	4,000	0	0	0
Charges paid						
Gift aid donation	4,000	4,500	2,000	5,000	0	0

Required

(a) Compute the MCT payable for the above accounting period by each of the above companies, assuming group relief is claimed, where appropriate, in the most efficient manner.

(b) Advise the board of P Ltd of the advantages of increasing its holding in S Ltd, a company likely to sustain trading losses for the next two years before becoming profitable.

Guidance notes

1   Group relief questions nearly always require you to show the most efficient use of relief. You must work out the profits of each company involved, and consider the marginal tax rate of each company. Any company with small companies' marginal relief will have a marginal rate (for FY 2002) of 32.75%. Any company with starting rate marginal relief will have a marginal rate of 23.75% for FY 2002.

2   Before working out the rates of tax, you must find the lower and upper limits for small companies rate, the starting rate and marginal relief. These depend on the number of companies under common control.

3   You must also remember that eligibility for group relief depends not on common control, but on a 75% effective interest.

20   PREPARATION QUESTION: CORRESPONDING ACCOUNTING PERIODS

Harry Ltd owns 80% of the ordinary share capital of Sid Ltd. Neither company has any other associated companies and both companies have been trading since 1987.

The following information relates to the two most recent accounting periods of each company.

Harry Ltd	12 months to 31.12.01	9 months to 30.9.02
Income	£	£
Schedule D Case I/(loss)	25,000	(45,000)
Schedule A	3,000	4,000
Charges paid		
Gift aid donation	2,000	2,000

Sid Ltd	12 months to 31.3.02	12 months to 31.3.03
Income	£	£
Schedule D Case I	52,000	250,000
Schedule D Case III	8,000	10,000
Charges paid		
Gift aid donation	5,000	5,000

Required

Compute the MCT payable by each company for each of the above accounting periods and show any loss carried forward by Harry Ltd on the assumption that Harry Ltd surrenders as much of its loss to Sid Ltd as is permitted and Harry Ltd does not make any claim to set its loss against its own profits.

Guidance notes

1   The general rule for group relief is that the profits and the losses which are to be matched up must have arisen at the same time.

2   To apply this rule where companies do not have matching accounting periods, time-apportionment must be used to work out the profits and losses of each period covered by accounting periods of the two companies. Time-apportionment is not, however, used when a company joins or leaves a group if the result would be unjust or unreasonable.

3   You may find the following table helpful.

Common period	Harry Ltd	Sid Ltd
1.1.02 – 31.3.02	(1.1.02 – 30.9.02) × 3/9	(1.4.01 – 31.3.02) × 3/12
1.4.02 – 30.9.02	(1.1.02 – 30.9.02) × 6/9	(1.4.02 – 31.3.03) × 6/12

4   The small companies rate was 20% for FY 99/FY 2000/FY 2001. The marginal relief fraction was 1/40. For FY 2002 the small companies rate is 19%, the small companies marginal relief fraction is 11/400.

21   A LTD   *27 mins*

On 1 July 2002 A Ltd, a manufacturing company resident in the United Kingdom, acquired 100% of the share capital of B Ltd, also a manufacturing company. B Ltd makes up accounts each year to 30 June. For its year ended 30 June 2003, it sustained a trading loss of £130,000 and had no other chargeable income. A Ltd produced the following information in relation to its nine-month period of accounts to 31 December 2002.

INCOME	£
Adjusted trading profits	42,000
Rents receivable	13,000
Loan interest receivable (received gross)	8,000
(including £2,000 accrued at 31 December 2002)	
Bank interest receivable	5,000
(including £3,000 accrued: £2,000 received 30 June 2002)	
Franked investment income (FII)	1,000
(including tax credit received August 2002)	
Charges Paid:	
Gift aid payment (paid September 2002)	17,000

Required

Compute the final taxation position of A Ltd for the above accounting period, assuming maximum group relief is claimed by A Ltd in respect of B Ltd's trading loss.

State the due date for payment of the corporation tax and the date by which A Ltd must file a corporation tax return in respect of the above period. **(15 marks)**

22 APPLE LTD (PILOT PAPER) *27 mins*

Apple Ltd owns 100% of the ordinary share capital of Banana Ltd and Cherry Ltd. The results of each company for the year ended 31 March 2003 are as follows:

	Apple Ltd £	*Banana Ltd* £	*Cherry Ltd* £
Tax adjusted Schedule DI profit/(loss)	(125,000)	650,000	130,000
Capital gain/(loss)	188,000	(8,000)	-

Apple Ltd's capital gain arose from the sale of a freehold warehouse on 15 April 2002 for £418,000. Cherry Ltd purchased a freehold office building for £290,000 on 10 January 2003.

Required

(a) Explain the group relationship that must exist in order that group relief can be claimed. (3 marks)

(b) Explain how group relief should be allocated between the respective claimant companies in order to maximise the potential benefit obtained from the relief.(4 marks)

(c) Assuming that reliefs are claimed in the most favourable manner, calculate the corporation tax liabilities of Apple Ltd, Banana Ltd and Cherry Ltd for the year ended 31 March 2003. (8 marks)

(15 marks)

23 ALPHABETIC LTD *27 mins*

(a) Alphabetic Ltd makes up annual accounts to 30 September. It paid four quarterly instalments of corporation tax of £156,000 each in respect of the accounting period to 30 September 2002. These were paid on 14 April 2002, 14 July 2002, 14 October 2002 and 14 January 2003. It subsequently transpired that the actual liability for the period was £800,000 and the balance of £176,000 was subsequently paid on 1 July 2003.

Alphabetic Ltd has always paid corporation tax at the full rate.

Required

State the amounts on which interest will be charged in respect of the above accounting period and the dates from which it will run. (4 marks)

(b) You are required to state what action a company should take if it does not receive a corporation tax return and the penalty for not taking such action. (2 marks)

(c) You are required to state:

    (i)   the fixed rate penalties for failing to submit a corporation tax return on time; and (4 marks)

    (ii)   the tax-geared penalties for failing to submit a corporation tax return on time. (3 marks)

Your answers to (c)(i) and (c)(ii) should indicate under what circumstances these penalties are triggered.

(d) Large companies must normally pay their corporation tax liability by instalments. State the circumstances in which such a company does not need to make instalment payments. (2 marks)

(15 marks)

24   PREPARATION QUESTION: COMPUTING VAT DUE

A company which is registered for VAT but does not use the cash accounting scheme has the following transactions in the quarter from July to September 2002. All amounts exclude any VAT.

	£
Bought computers for resale	130,000
Sold computers	210,000
Bought books about computers	9,300
Sold books about computers	8,400
Wrote off a bad debt in respect of a standard rated sale for which payment was due in January 2002	4,000

The sales of computers are stated at their full value before any settlement discount. However, £20,000 of the sales were subject to a 5% discount for payment within 30 days. The discount was taken up in respect of half of those sales.

Required

Calculate the VAT due on 31 October 2002.

Guidance notes

1   First identify the standard rated purchases and sales, and the zero rated purchases and sales.

2   Then consider the effect of the settlement discount. Does it matter whether it is taken up?

3   Then compute the VAT on standard rated purchases and sales.

4   Finally, VAT will have been accounted for on the sale in January. Is any relief available?

25   NEWCOMER LTD, ONGOING LTD AND AU REVOIR LTD (PILOT PAPER)   *27 mins*

(a) Newcomer Ltd commenced trading on 1 October 2002. Its forecast sales are as follows.

		£
2002	October	9,500
	November	14,200
	December	21,400
2003	January	12,300
	February	14,700
	March	15,200

The company's sales are all standard rated, and the above figures are exclusive of VAT.

Required

Explain when Newcomer Ltd will be required to compulsorily register for VAT.(4 marks)

(b) Ongoing Ltd is registered for VAT, and its sales are all standard rated. The following information relates to the company's VAT return for the quarter ended 30 September 2002:

(1)   Standard rated sales amounted to £120,000. Ongoing Ltd offers its customers a 5% discount for prompt payment, and this discount is taken by half of the customers.

(2)   Standard rated purchases and expenses amounted to £35,640. This figure includes £480 for entertaining customers.

(3)   On 15 September 2002 the company wrote off bad debts of £2,000 and £840 in respect of invoices due for payment on 10 February and 5 May 2002 respectively.

(4)   On 30 September 2002 the company purchased a motor car at a cost of £16,450 for the use of a salesperson, and machinery at a cost of £21,150. Both these figures are inclusive of VAT. The motor car is used for both business and private mileage.

Unless stated otherwise, all of the above figures are exclusive of VAT. Ongoing Ltd does not operate the cash accounting scheme.

Required

Calculate the amount of VAT payable by Ongoing Ltd for the quarter ended 30 September 2002.   (8 marks)

(c)   Au Revoir Ltd has been registered for VAT since 1994, and its sales are all standard rated. The company has recently seen a downturn in its business activities, and sales for the years ended 31 October 2002 and 2003 are forecast to be £55,000 and £47,500 respectively. Both of these figures are exclusive of VAT.

Required

Explain why Au Revoir Ltd will be permitted to voluntarily deregister for VAT, and from what date registration will be effective.   (3 marks)

(15 marks)

> **TAXATION OF UNINCORPORATED BUSINESSES**
>
> Question 26 to 42 cover the taxation of unincorporated businesses, the subject of Part B of the BPP Study Text for Paper 2.3.

26   SELF ASSESSMENT FOR INDIVIDUALS

27 mins

(a)   You are required to state the latest date by which an individual taxpayer should submit the tax return if:

    (i)   he wishes the Inland Revenue to calculate his income tax liability; and

    (ii)   he wishes to calculate his own liability.   (4 marks)

(b)   You are required to state:

    (i)   the normal dates of payment of Schedule DI and II income tax for a sole trader in respect of the fiscal year 2002/03; and

    (ii)   how the amounts of these payments are arrived at.   (5 marks)

(c)   You are required to state the circumstances in which a payment on account is not required to be made by a taxpayer.   (2 marks)

(d)   You are required to state:

    (i)   the fixed penalties for late submission of tax returns and when they apply;

    (ii)   the circumstances under which the penalties will be reduced; and

    (iii) the further penalties which may be imposed where the Inland Revenue believe that the fixed penalties will not result in the submission of the return. (4 marks)

(15 marks)

27   ENQUIRIES AND DETERMINATIONS

27 mins

The Inland Revenue have to give written notice before the commencement of an enquiry into the completeness and accuracy of a self-assessment tax return.

Required

(a)   State the date by which this written notice must normally be issued;   (1 mark)

(b)   State the circumstances under which the Inland Revenue can extend the deadline in (a) within which an enquiry may be commenced together with the relevant time limits;   (5 marks)

(c)   State the three main reasons for the commencement of an enquiry;   (3 marks)

(d)   State what choices are open to the taxpayer where he has been notified by the Inland Revenue that there is an additional liability as a result of an enquiry; and   (2 marks)

(e)   State what is meant by a determination and the time limit for making one.   (4 marks)

(15 marks)

28 MADELAINE AND OTTO

27 mins

(a) Madelaine has for many years been in business as a furniture and carpet retailer. Her trading and profit and loss account for the year ended 31 March 2003 is as follows.

	£	£
Sales		89,323
Opening stock	26,544	
Purchases	23,338	
	49,882	
Closing stock	24,628	
		(25,254)
Gross profit		64,069
Wages and national insurance	15,197	
Repairs and renewals	491	
Rent and rates	13,984	
General expenses	719	
Bad debts	955	
Depreciation of fixtures and fittings	415	
Interest	1,780	
Motor vehicle running costs	1,404	
Lighting and heating	2,954	
Re-location expenses	741	
Professional fees	645	
Subscriptions and donations	194	
		39,479
Net profit		24,590

Required

State what additional information you would need in order to calculate Madelaine's tax adjusted Schedule D Case I profit for the year ended 31 March 2003 and explain why you need it. (9 marks)

(b) Otto is a self-employed television engineer. He commenced in business on 1 June 1999 and initially made up accounts to 30 November but has now changed his accounting date to 28 February.

Otto's recent results have been:

	£
1.6.99 – 30.11.99	7,000
1.12.99 – 30.11.00	16,000
1.12.00 – 30.11.01	19,000
1.12.01 – 28.2.03	25,000

Required

Calculate the amounts chargeable to income tax under Schedule D, Case I for the years 1999/00, 2000/01, 2001/02 and 2002/03. (6 marks)

(15 marks)

29 MALCOLM

27 mins

(a) Malcolm started in business as a self-employed builder on 1 August 2001. His adjusted trading results, after capital allowances, were:

	£
Period ended 30.11.01	(10,000) Loss
Year ended 30.11.02	(20,000) Loss
Year ended 30.11.03	15,000 Profit

Prior to being self-employed Malcolm was employed as a builder when his earnings were:

	£
2001/02 (to 31 July 2001)	5,650
2000/01	8,000

He received annual building society interest income of £3,040 (net) from 2000/01 onwards. In 2001/02 he realised a capital gain on the disposal of a non business asset of £7,900 after indexation but before the annual exemption. Taper relief was not available on the disposal of this non business asset.

Required

Show how Malcolm's trading losses can be utilised most effectively, giving your reasoning.

You may assume the 2002/03 rates and allowances apply to all years relevant to this question.   (12 marks)

(b) You are required to state by what date(s) the claims you are proposing in part (a) should be submitted to the Inland Revenue.   (3 marks)

(15 marks)

30   JACQUELINE   *27 mins*

Jacqueline retired from her 'Do-it-yourself' shop on 30 September 2002. She had commenced trading on 1 May 1998 and had prepared accounts to 31 December each year.

Her adjusted profits/loss had been agreed with the Inland Revenue as follows.

	£
Period to 31.12.98	5,000 profit
Year ended 31.12.99	8,000 profit
Year ended 31.12.00	13,000 profit
Year ended 31.12.01	10,000 profit
Period to 30.09.02	14,500 loss

Required

(a) Show the Schedule D Case I profits for 1998/99 to 2002/03 before claiming relief for the loss.   (5 marks)

(b) Show the final Schedule D Case I profits for 1998/99 to 2002/03 after claiming terminal loss relief.   (10 marks)

(15 marks)

31   PREPARATION QUESTION: PARTNERSHIPS

Clare and Justin commenced trading in partnership on 1 October 1999, initially sharing profits and losses as to Clare one third and Justin two thirds. They prepared their first set of accounts to 31 January 2000. Accounts were prepared to 31 January thereafter.

Malcolm joined the partnership on 1 May 2001. From this date the profit and losses were shared equally. On 31 December 2002, Justin resigned with Clare and Malcolm continuing to share profits equally. Schedule D Case I profits were as follows:

	£
1.10.99 - 31.01.00	26,400
y/e 31.01.01	60,000
y/e 31.01.02	117,000
y/e 31.01.03	108,108

Required

Calculate the amount on which each partner will be taxed in respect of the partnership profits for 1999/00 to 2002/03 inclusive. Show any overlap profits that remain unrelieved.

Guidance notes

1   You should start by dividing the profits for each period of account between the partners in accordance with the profit sharing ratio for that period.

2   Next you can work out how much profit should be taxed in each tax year. Apply the opening and closing year rules to each partner individually according to when he or she joins or leaves the partnership.

3   Each partner has their own overlap profits. These can be relieved when the partner concerned leaves the partnership (or possibly, on an earlier change of accounting date).

32   ROGER AND BRIGITTE   *27 mins*

Roger and Brigitte commenced in business on 1 October 1998 as hotel proprietors, sharing profits equally.

On 1 October 2000 their son Xavier joined the partnership and from that date each of the partners was entitled to one-third of the profits.

The profits of the partnership adjusted for income tax, are:

	£
Period ended 30 June 1999	30,000
Year ended 30 June 2000	45,000
Year ended 30 June 2001	50,000
Year ended 30 June 2002	60,000

Required

(a)   Calculate the assessable profits on each of the partners for all relevant years from 1998/99 to 2002/03; and   (11 marks)

(b)   Calculate the overlap profits for each of the partners.   (4 marks)

(15 marks)

33   PARTNERSHIPS (PILOT PAPER)   *27 mins*

(a)   *Required*

Briefly explain the basis by which partners are assessed in respect of their share of a partnership's Schedule DI or DII profit.   (3 marks)

(b)   Anne and Betty have been in partnership since 1 January 1997 sharing profits equally. On 30 June 2002 Betty resigned as a partner, and was replaced on 1 July 2002 by Chloe. Profit continued to be shared equally. The partnership's Schedule DI profits are as follows:

	£
Year ended 31 December 2002	60,000
Year ended 31 December 2003	72,000

As at 6 April 2002 Anne and Betty each have unrelieved overlap profits of £3,000.

Put-it-Right plc paid for the petrol in respect of all the mileage done by Lai during 2002/03. She paid the company £30 per month towards the cost of her private petrol.

The motor car was returned to Put-it-Right plc on 31 December 2002.

(4) Put-it-Right plc provided Lai with an interest free loan of £30,000 on 1 January 1999. She repaid £20,000 of the loan on 30 June 2002 with the balance of £10,000 being repaid on 31 December 2002. The loan was not used for a qualifying purposes.

On 1 January 2003 Lai commenced in self-employment running a music recording studio. The following information relates to the period of self-employment from 1 January to 5 April 2003.

(1) The Schedule DII profit for the period 1 January to 5 April 2003 is £19,900. This figure is *before* taking account of capital allowances.

(2) Lai purchased the following assets:

1 January 2003	Recording equipment	£9,300
15 January 2003	Motor car	£14,800
20 February 2003	Motor car	£10,400
4 March 2003	Recording equipment	£2,600

The motor car purchased on 15 January 2003 for £14,800 is used by Lai, and 40% of the mileage is for private purposes. The motor car purchased on 20 February 2003 for £10,400 is used by an employee, and 10% of the mileage is for private purposes.

The recording equipment purchased on 4 March 2003 for £2,600 is to be treated as a short-life asset.

(3) Since becoming self-employed Lai has paid £390 (net) per month into a stakeholder pension scheme. Payments are made on the 20th of each month.

(4) Lai Chan is single and does not have any children.

Required

(a) Calculate Lai's income tax liability for 2002/03. (20 marks)

(b) Briefly explain how Lai's income tax liability for 2002/03 will be paid to the Inland Revenue. (5 marks)

(25 marks)

37 **CLAYTON DELANEY** *47 mins*

Clayton Delaney, who is now aged 59, had been a self-employed electrician for many years. His business was centred on a shop from which he sold electrical goods to the public and to the electrical trade. He also carried out electrical work himself for his customers.

Because of deteriorating health his wife could no longer look after the shop in Clayton's absence and she retired aged 60 on 31 March 2002. She had no source of income thereafter. Clayton decided to permanently cease trading on 30 June 2002 and on 1 July 2002 commenced working for a firm of electrical contractors.

His summarised accounts for the year ended 30 June 2002 are as follows.

Profit and loss account

		£			£
Telephone	(1)	240	Gross profits on sales *receiveable*		19,645
Repairs	(2)	1,180	Bank interest received (Note (3)		300
Depreciation		1,350	of other relevant information)		
Buildings insurance	(3)	600	Profit on sale of shop fittings		20
Lighting and heating	(3)	420	Work done for customers		16,000
Car expenses	(4)	1,750			
Bad debts	(5)	950			
Rates	(6)	1,850			
Wages and national					
insurance contributions:					
Mrs Delaney	(7)	5,000			
Wages and national					
insurance contributions:					
Mr Delaney		11,850			
Bank interest paid	(8)	630			
General expenses	(9)	1,995			
Net profit		8,150			
		35,965			35,965

Figures in brackets refers to notes to the accounts.

Notes to the accounts

(1) Telephone: one-fifth of the charge is for private calls.

(2) Repairs were as follows (see also note (3)).

	£
Roof repairs	650
Redecorating bedroom	230
Replacing floor tiles in shop	300
	1,180

(3) Clayton and his wife live on the shop premises. The Inland Revenue have agreed that two-thirds of the household expenditure is in respect of the living accommodation.

(4) Car expenses: the total mileage in the year was 16,000 of which half was private. This was the same fraction as in earlier years.

(5) **Bad debts**

	£		£
Trade debts written off	300	Specific debt provision b/f	300
Loan to neighbour written off	500	Recovery of trade debt	
Specific debt provision c/f	800	previously written off	350
		Profit and loss account	950
	1,600		1,600

(6) **Rates**

	£
Business rates	1,200
Council tax	650
	1,850

(7) Mrs Delaney's wages: Mrs Delaney looked after the shop in Mr Delaney's absence and ran the clerical side of the business.

(8) Bank interest paid: the interest was paid on the business account overdraft.

(9) **General expenses**

	£
Accountancy	600
Legal costs in defending claim for allegedly faulty work	200
Printing, stationery and postage	220
Gifts to trade customers: one Christmas hamper each, costing £30	900
Donation of prize in local carnival (a free advertisement was provided in the programme)	50
Donation to a national charity (not paid under the gift aid scheme)	25
	1,995

(10) Overlap profits on commencement of trade were £1,200.

In addition Clayton had taken stock from the shop for personal use. The cost price of these items was £600 and the average gross profit margin was 20%. No payment had been made for the goods by Clayton.

The tax written-down values at 1 July 2001 of business assets were as follows.

Car	£5,700
Pool	£490

On 31 December 2001 Clayton traded in his car for £4,500 and purchased a new one costing £9,000.

On 30 June 2002 the items in the pool were sold for £400 (all less than original cost) and the car had a market value of £3,500.

Other relevant information is as follows.

(1) Clayton earned £1,433.33 gross per month, payable on the last day of the month in arrears. Because he was expected to travel around in his employment he was provided with a company car by his employer.

(2) The car had a diesel engine with a capacity of 1,300 cc and had a list price of £10,000 when new. Its CO_2 emissions were 172g/km. Clayton's employer agreed to provide fuel for the first 5,000 miles of his private motoring during 2002/03.

(3) Clayton has an investment account with the Halifax Bank. Interest of £395 was credited on 31 December 2002.

(4) Clayton had purchased a life annuity and received a monthly gross amount of £100 on the first of each month commencing 1 September 2002. The capital element of the payment was agreed by the Revenue to be £50 per month. The income element of the annuity was received net of 20% tax.

Required

(a) Calculate the amount of the taxable profits for 2002/03.   (19 marks)

(b) Calculate the amount of Clayton's income tax payable for 2002/03.   (7 marks)

(26 marks)

38   BRUCE   *45 mins*

Bruce died on 31 May 2002 when he was 61. His wife Madeline had died several years earlier.

Bruce had the following income in 2002/03, up to his death.

	£
Retirement pension	800
Income from employment (PAYE deducted £380)	3,385
Dividends (net)	10,125
Capital gain on non-business asset bought in May 2000	
(prior to death, before annual exemption)	32,000
Bank interest (net)	40

No taper relief is due in respect of the chargeable gain.

Bruce's sister, Sheila, had started a wholesale soft furnishing business on 1 June 2000. The profits as adjusted for income tax, but before capital allowances, were as follows.

	£
1.6.00 - 30.4.01	13,500
1.5.01 - 30.4.02	20,000
Capital additions were:	
1.6.00 Car	8,500
4.8.00 Computer	1,000
1.10.01 Shelving and furniture	10,000

The car was also used by Sheila privately. The private mileage was 50% of the total mileage. Shiela's business qualified as a small enterprise for first year allowance purposes.

No claim is to be made to treat any of the assets as 'short-life' assets.

Sheila aged 57 paid a personal pension contribution of £3,200 (gross) in 2002/03.

Required

(a) Calculate any income tax and capital gains tax payable or repayable on Bruce's income and capital gains for 2002/03.   (12 marks)

(b) Calculate the Schedule D Case I income tax assessment on Sheila for the years 2000/01, 2001/02 and 2002/03.   (6 marks)

(c) Calculate Sheila's 'overlap' profits.   (1 mark)

(d) Calculate Sheila's income tax and Class 4 NIC liabilities for 2002/03.   (6 marks)

                                                                            (25 marks)

39   PREPARATION QUESTION: A COTTAGE AND SHARES

John Hammond, a single man aged 60, had Schedule E income of £8,000, dividend income of £16,200 net and had the following transactions in the year ended 5 April 2003.

(a) On 5 May 2002 he sold his holiday cottage in Scotland for £100,000. The legal and advertising expenses of the sale were £800.

John had purchased the property on 5 September 1982 for £25,000 and had incurred costs of £8,000 on 1 December 1983 for the building of an extension.

(b) On 14 September 2002 he sold 4,000 shares in JVD Products plc for £40,000, his previous transactions being as follows.

12 June 1986 purchased 700 shares cost £3,000
12 May 1999 purchased 2,800 shares cost £12,000
12 August 2001 purchased 500 shares cost £2,000

The shares are a non-business asset for taper relief purposes.

Required

Compute the income tax and capital gains tax liabilities of John Hammond for the year 2002/03.

Guidance notes

1 The key date to remember in any CGT question is 6 April 1998.

2 It is important to set out a CGT calculation in the right way.

3 Individuals do not get an indexation allowance after 6 April 1998. Instead they may be eligible for taper relief.

4 Shares acquired after 6.4.98 are not pooled. They are matched with disposals on a LIFO basis. In this question you are not given indexation factors so you must work them out from first principles.

5 When you come to work out the tax liabilities, remember that income and gains share the starting and basic rate bands. Income is dealt with first then any gains in the starting rate band are taxed at 10%. Any gains in the basic rate band are taxed at 20%. Gains that fall into the higher rate band are taxed at 40%.

40 YVONNE, SALLY AND JOANNE *27 mins*

(a) Yvonne had the following transactions in the shares of Scotia plc. The shares are a non business asset for taper relief purposes.

		Shares	£
18 August 1995	bought	3,000	6,000
19 September 2000	bought	2,000	5,000
13 March 2003	sold	5,000	23,000
28 March 2003	bought	1,000	4,400

(Indexation factor August 1995 - April 1998 is 0.085)

You are required to calculate Yvonne's capital gain for 2002/03. (8 marks)

(b) In 2002/03 Sally's capital gains tax position was as follows.

	£
Capital gain on a business asset qualifying for 25% taper relief	40,000
Capital gain on non-business asset*	10,000
Capital loss arising in year	6,000
Capital loss brought forward	12,000

* The non-business asset does not qualify for taper relief in 2002/03.

Required

Show how the losses should be allocated to obtain the maximum tax advantage and calculate any gain chargeable. (4 marks)

(c) Joanne bought a warehouse for use in her business on 1 August 2000. She used it until 1 August 2001 and then let it out until she sold it on 1 February 2003. Her gain on sale was £50,000.

Required

Show Joanne's gain after taper relief. (3 marks)

(15 marks)

35

41 SUSAN WHITE (PILOT PAPER)   *27 mins*

Susan White disposed of the following assets during 2002/03.

1   On 15 July 2002 Susan sold 20,000 £1 ordinary shares in Red Ltd for £55,000. Susan bought 25,000 shares in the company on 2 June 2001 for £37,500. She bought a further 5,000 shares on 18 July 2002 for £15,000.

2   On 25 August 2002 Susan sold 50,000 £1 ordinary shares in Blue Ltd to her son for £70,000. The market value of the shares on this date was £200,000. The shareholding was purchased on 15 April 1985 for £18,000. Take the indexation allowance from April 1985 to April 1998 to be £12,800. Susan and her son are to elect to hold over the gain as a gift of a business asset.

Red Ltd and Blue Ltd are unquoted trading companies. Susan's shareholding in each company qualifies as a business asset for the purposes of CGT taper relief.

Required

(a) Describe the types of shareholding that qualify as a business asset for the purposes of CGT taper relief.   (4 marks)

(b) Calculate the capital gains arising from Susan's disposal during 2002/03. You should ignore the annual exemption.   (11 marks)

(15 marks)

42 MR EDWARDS   *27 mins*

A client, Mr Edwards, has made an appointment to discuss his VAT position with you on 10 December 2002. He started in business making hand-made ladies' shoes on 1 April 2002. His monthly turnover figures to date are:

	£
April	5,694
May	5,326
June	7,295
July	7,314
August	9,405
September	10,792
October	10,977
November	11,291

Turnover is expected to continue to increase. Mr Edwards is concerned that he should now be charging customers VAT and is seeking your advice about registration.

He has heard that if he has to register for VAT he can submit an annual return to cut down on administration.

He would welcome your advice on both these matters.

Required

Prepare notes for your meeting with Mr Edwards.   **(15 marks)**

EMPLOYEES

Questions 43 to 46 cover employees, the subject of Part C of the BPP Study Text for Paper 2.3.

43   PREPARATION QUESTION: BENEFITS

You have been asked to assist in the completion of forms P11D in respect of the directors of your company for the year 2002/03.

The following benefits are enjoyed by various directors.

(a)   A director has had the use of a private house bought by the company for £120,000 in 1999. The director paid all of the house expenses plus the agreed open market annual rental of £2,000. The annual value of the house is £2,000.

(b)   A television video system, which had been provided at the start of 1998/99 for the use of a director and which had cost the company £3,500, was taken over by the director on 6 April 2002 for a payment of £600 (its market value at that date).

(c)   A director has a loan of £4,000 at 4% interest to enable him to purchase his annual season ticket. This is the only loan he had taken out.

(d)   Medical insurance premiums were paid for a director and his family, under a group scheme, at a cost to the company of £800. Had the director paid for this as an individual the cost would have been £1,400.

(e)   On 6 September 2002 a director was given the use of a Mercedes car which had cost £24,000. The CO_2 emissions of the car were 265g/km. The director used the Mercedes for both business and private purposes. He was required to make good the cost of any petrol used for private mileage.

(f)   On 6 April 2002 the company lent a director a computer costing £3,900 for use at home. The director used the computer for both business and private purposes.

Required

Show how each of the above benefits would be quantified for inclusion in the forms P11D. Assume that the official rate of interest is 5%.

Guidance notes

1   Work through each benefit separately. Calculate its value before you move on to the next benefit. Watch out for exempt benefits.

2   Remember that any benefit that is only available for part of a year must be time apportioned. This is often the case in exam questions with car and fuel benefits. Is it relevant here?

3   The rules for the calculation of car benefits changed from 6.4.02. Ensure you can deal with the new rules as they are extremely topical.

44   RITA   *27 mins*

Rita, who is a fashion designer for Daring Designs Limited, was re-located from London to Manchester on 6 April 2002. Her annual salary is £48,000. She was immediately provided with a house with an annual value of £4,000 for which her employer paid an annual rent of £3,500. Rita was re-imbursed relevant re-location expenditure of £12,000. Daring Designs Limited provided ancillary services for the house in 2002/03 as follows.

	£
Electricity	700
Gas	1,200
Water	500
Council tax	1,300
Property repairs	3,500

The house has been furnished by Daring Designs Limited prior to Rita's occupation at a cost of £30,000. On 6 October 2002 Rita bought all of the furniture from Daring Designs Ltd for £20,000 when its market value was £25,000.

Daring Designs Limited had made an interest free loan to Rita in 2001 of £10,000. The loan is not being used for a 'qualifying purpose'. No part of the loan has been repaid.

Rita was provided with a 1,800cc company car. It had a list price of £18,500 and a CO_2 emissions figure of 169g/km. Daring Designs Limited paid for the petrol for all the mileage done by Rita until 5 December 2002. On 5 December 2002 the company discontinued the company car scheme and sold the car to Rita for £5,000, its market value on that date.

Required

Calculate the total amount chargeable to income tax under Schedule E on Rita for the year 2002/03.

(15 marks)

45 JOSEPHINE
27 mins

Josephine, who is not contracted out of the state pension scheme, receives a weekly salary of £402. Josephine is provided with a company car by her employer. Until 5 December 2002 the car was a 1900 cc diesel car with CO_2 emissions of 201g/km. The original list price of this car was £12,000. On 6 December 2002 the car was exchanged for a new 2,500 cc petrol car with a list price of £21,000 and a CO_2 emissions figure of 168g/km. Josephine's employer provided fuel for both cars for both business and private motoring.

Josephine also received the benefit of medical insurance at the cost of £500 to her employer. Her employer also paid £10,000 to a private nursery for places for Josephine's two small children under a contract between the employer and the nursery.

Required

Calculate the national insurance contributions payable by Josephine and her employer for the year 2002/03.

(15 marks)

46 MR K
27 mins

Mr K is the managing director of Q Ltd. The company provides him with a number of benefits in kind in addition to his salary of £60,000 per annum.

For 2002/03 these benefits comprise:

(a) *Motor cars*

Mr K was given the use of a Mercedes car which had cost the company £24,000 and had CO_2 emissions of 167g/km. On 5 August 2002, Mr K was involved in a serious accident in which the Mercedes was totally destroyed. Mr K was injured and did not drive or return to work until 5 October 2002.

On his return to work on 5 October 2002, he was provided with a Lexus motor car which cost the company £36,000. The CO_2 emissions of the car was 217g/km.

As a result of the car crash, Mr K was found guilty of dangerous driving and the company paid his legal costs and fine amounting to £1,200 with Mr K making a contribution of £300.

Mr K was provided with petrol for both cars by the company, including that used for private mileage. The fuel benefits for 2002/03 for both the cars is £4,200 per annum.

(b) *Suits*

Mr K was provided, for the whole of the tax year, with two suits of clothes, each costing £800.

(c) *Housing*

Mr K lived in a house owned by the company, which bought it last year for £125,000. The annual rental value was £8,000 and Mr K paid rent of £5,000 to the company.

The company is currently considering, for the first time, paying annual cash bonuses to its directors.

Required

(a) Compute the total value of the benefits assessable on Mr K for the year 2002/03. Assume the official rate of interest is 5%.   (7 marks)

(b) Compute any additional cost to be met by the company as a result of providing the above benefits.   (2 marks)

(c) Draft a short memo to the board explaining the method of taxing bonuses paid to directors and indicating how the tax will be accounted for.   (6 marks)

                                                                          (15 marks)

47 ERICA

27 mins

Erica has been offered two jobs and is wondering which one to take. In order to help her reach her decision, she has asked your advice about the income tax and national insurance position. Erica has no other income.

The remuneration packages on offer are as follows:

Employer A

A salary of £25,000. A bonus of 5% of salary if Erica meets certain targets (Erica is sure she will do so).

Erica will be required use her car for business. It is a 1,400cc Peugeot 206. The employer will pay a mileage allowance of 50p per mile. Erica expects to travel 3,000 miles on business per year.

Employer B

A salary of £22,000.

Erica will be provided with a new company car (1,400 cc) with a list price of £12,000 and a CO_2 emissions figure of 219g/km. She will be provided with all her petrol, for both business and private use.

Erica will be provided with a computer which she can use for business and private use. The computer will cost £2,000.

Erica will also be provided with an interest free loan to buy her rail season ticket. The cost of the ticket is £2,000. The loan will be paid back in monthly instalments.

Erica will be eligible to join her employer's group private medical insurance scheme at a cost to the employer of £750 per year.

Required

Calculate the net income per year that Erica will have if she takes the job with

(a) Employer A; or	(6 marks)
(b) Employer B	(9 marks)

after income tax and national insurance. **(15 marks)**

48 SASHA SHAH (PILOT PAPER)

27 mins

Sasha Shah is a computer programmer. Until 5 April 2002 she was employed by Net Computers plc, but since then has worked independently from home. Sasha's income for the year ended 5 April 2003 is £60,000. All of this relates to work done for Net Computers plc. Her expenditure for the year ended 5 April 2003 is as follows:

(1) The business proportion of light, heat and telephone for Sasha's home is £600.

(2) Computer equipment was purchased on 6 April 2002 for £8,000.

(3) A motor car was purchased on 6 April 2002 for £10,000. Motor expenses for the year ended 6 April 2003 amount to £3,500, of which 40% relate to journeys between home and the premises of Net Computers plc. The other 60% relate to private mileage.

Required

(a)   List eight factors that will indicate that a worker should be treated as an employee rather than as self-employed.   (4 marks)

(b)   (i)   Calculate Sasha's liability to Class 2 and Class 4 NIC if she is treated as self-employed during 2002/03.

(ii)   Calculate Sasha's liability to Class 1 NIC if she is treated as an employee during 2002/03.   (4 marks)

(c)   (i)   Calculate the amount of income assessable under Schedule DII if Sasha is treated as self-employed during 2002/03.

(ii)   Calculate the amount of income assessable under Schedule E if Sasha is treated as an employee during 2002/03.   (7 marks)

(15 marks)

49   MR ROYLE   *27 mins*

Your client, Mr Royle, is considering acquiring the business of a local company. The company has previously been profitable but has made losses in the last two years due to the ill-health of the managing director, who is also the main shareholder. Mr Royle is sure that he can turn the business around and make it profitable again. The company owns various items of machinery and a factory.

Mr Royle is considering either buying the assets of the company or buying the whole of the shares in the company. He was made redundant by his employer last year and received a large cash payment which he will be using to buy the business.

Required

Write a letter to Mr Royle outlining the advantages and disadvantages of buying:

(a)   the assets of the business; or   (8 marks)
(b)   the shares in the company.   (7 marks)

(15 marks)

50   MRS DOUGLAS   *27 mins*

(a)   Mrs Douglas is the sole shareholder and director of Zeta Ltd. The company is estimated to make a profit of £30,000 in the year to 31 March 2003 (after paying out the salary below). It has no corporation tax liability due to the use of losses from previous years.

Mrs Douglas has received a salary of £4,800 in 2002/03 from the company. She has no other sources of income.

Required

Calculate the net amount of income after tax and national insurance from the company in the hands of Mrs Douglas for 2002/03 if:

(i)   the company pays her a bonus of £10,000 on 1 April 2003; or   (5 marks)
(ii)   the company pays her a dividend of £10,000 on 1 April 2003.   (7 marks)

(b) Mrs Douglas has enquired whether it would be more advantageous for her not to receive any salary from Zeta Ltd next year, but simply a dividend of £15,000. The company is likely to make a profit next year and will be liable to corporation tax.

Required

State whether such a course of action would be advantageous. Assume the rates and rules of tax in 2002/03 also apply in 2003/04. (3 marks)

(15 marks)

Answers

1 PREPARATION QUESTION: SUNDRY ADJUSTMENTS

> **Pass marks**. The factory had always been used as a factory, so you should not have discussed the effect of non-qualifying use.

(a) The gross amount of loan interest accruing during the year will be included in the company's profits chargeable to corporation tax and charged to tax at the appropriate rate. **The gross interest is taxed under schedule D case III on an accruals basis.**

(b) **There will be a charge to corporation tax on any capital gain.** In addition, the residue before sale must be calculated, being the cost less any industrial buildings allowances to date. **If the proceeds exceed the residue before sale a balancing charge will arise** (restricted to the amount of the allowances claimed) and will be chargeable to corporation tax. **If the proceeds are less than the residue before sale, the difference will give rise to a balancing allowance which will be added to the company's other capital allowances.**

(c) The **defalcations by the junior members of staff will be deductible** in arriving at the company's Schedule D Case I profits, provided that they are not covered by insurance. **Sums stolen by a director are not deductible** as a trading expense *(Bamford v ATA Advertising 1972)*.

(d) **Expenditure on repairs to a newly-acquired asset which cannot be used by the purchaser in its unaltered state is regarded as capital expenditure and is therefore not deductible in arriving at the company's Schedule D Case I profit** *(Law Shipping Co Ltd v CIR 1923)*. Furthermore, as the expenditure was on retail premises it will not qualify for industrial buildings allowances either.

(e) **The cost of business entertainment is not deductible** for tax purposes. **The cost of staff entertainment, on the other hand, is deductible.**

2 PREPARATION QUESTION: CAPITAL AND REVENUE

> **Pass marks**. The topic of this question is a basic principle of UK taxation. It would be very easy simply to write everything you know about the distinction between capital and revenue items. This would, however, be a mistake. It is important to read this sort of question carefully. You are asked how the distinction is applied to items in a company's profit and loss account, so you should consider profits as well as deductions from them, and you are specifically required to refer to relevant case law.

The distinction between capital and revenue is an essential one in the application of UK corporation tax. **Capital expenditure is not deductible in the computation of trading profits, except to the extent that it gives rise to capital allowances. Capital profits are taxed as capital gains:** although the rate of corporation tax is the same as for income, an indexation allowance is available in the computation of capital gains, and **capital losses may only be relieved against capital gains**.

Capital expenditure

Expenditure on an asset which is for the enduring benefit of the trade is capital. Thus the cost of a machine which will be used to generate profits is capital, but the cost of stock bought for resale is a revenue expense.

Legal and professional expenses associated with capital expenditure are themselves treated as capital. However, **the cost of registration of patents and trade marks, the cost of legal advice on employment contracts and the cost of legal work on the renewal of a**

lease for less than 50 years are all deductible in computing trading profits. The incidental costs of loan finance are deductible in that they are taken into account in computing profits and losses on loan relationships.

The most contentious items of expenditure will often be repairs (revenue expenditure) and improvements (capital expenditure). The distinction between the two is based on a number of important legal cases.

(a) **Restoration of an asset by, for instance, replacing a subsidiary part of the asset will be deductible expenditure**. It was held that expenditure on a replacement factory chimney was deductible since the chimney was a subsidiary part of the factory (*Samuel Jones & Co (Devondale) Ltd v CIR 1951*). However, in another case a football club demolished a spectators' stand and replaced it with a modern equivalent. This was held not to be repair, since repair is the restoration by renewal or replacement of subsidiary parts of a larger entity, and the stand formed a distinct and *separate* part of the club (and was thus not a *subsidiary* part of the club) (*Brown v Burnley Football and Athletic Co Ltd 1980*).

(b) **Initial repairs to improve a recently acquired asset to make it fit to earn profits will be treated as capital expenditure**. In *Law Shipping Co Ltd v CIR 1923* the taxpayer failed to obtain relief for expenditure on making a newly bought ship seaworthy prior to using it.

(c) **Initial repairs to remedy normal wear and tear of recently acquired assets will be deductible**. *Odeon Associated Theatres Ltd v Jones 1971* can be contrasted with the *Law Shipping* judgement. Odeon were allowed to deduct expenditure incurred on improving the state of recently acquired cinemas.

Where an asset is bought on hire purchase the cash cost is treated as capital, and the finance charges are treated as revenue expenditure, normally spread over the period of the hire purchase agreement. Where assets are leased, the lease payments are treated as revenue expenditure.

Capital profits

Where an asset is held to be used in the business (for example machinery) and is then sold, any profit is a capital gain. The same would apply to investments. Sales of stock in the course of trade, on the other hand, give rise to revenue profits.

3 TRUNK LTD

> **Pass marks**. In a question such as this, it is a good idea to tick each item on the question paper as you deal with it, so that you do not miss anything.

TRUNK LIMITED
COMPUTATION OF ADJUSTED PROFIT OR LOSS

	£	£	Note
Loss per accounts		(42,000)	
Additions to profit			
Lease premium amortisation	2,000		(a)
Depreciation	9,500		(a)
Loss on sale of lorry	6,000		(a)
Entertaining	1,800		(b)
Legal fees	4,400		(c)
General expenses	2,500		(d)
Repairs and renewals	5,000		(e)
		31,200	
		(10,800)	
Deductions from profit			
Reduction in general provision	1,000		(f)
Deemed extra rent	1,640		(g)
Rents received	10,000		(h)
Gain on sale of plant	7,400		(a)
Capital allowances	7,160		(i)
		(27,200)	
Adjusted loss		(38,000)	

Notes

(a) **Depreciation and amortisation are not deductible, being capital. Losses and gains on the sale of fixed assets** are essentially catching-up for inadequate or excessive depreciation, and **are similarly not deductible (losses) or taxable (gains)**.

(b) **The cost of entertaining customers, and the cost of gifts of food to customers, are by statute not deductible**. Entertaining staff is not caught by this rule.

(c) The **legal fees in relation to the new lease are not deductible** because they are capital in nature. The **legal fees in relation to the recovery of the employee loan are not deductible** because they are not for trade purposes: the trade is manufacturing, not moneylending. **Legal fees in relation to service contracts, are, however, deductible**.

(d) **Penalties and fines are not deductible**. Course fees for trade-related training of employees, on the other hand, are deductible.

(e) **The cost of the new windows is not deductible because it is of a capital nature,** being needed to put the recently-acquired warehouse in a usable condition. Routine repairs, on the other hand, are deductible.

(f) **General provisions are not deductible, so reductions in them are not taxable**. Specific provisions, on the other hand, and actual bad debts, are deductible.

(g) **When a trader pays a lease premium, the part treated as income for the landlord is treated as extra rent payable by the trader, spread over the term of the lease.** The extra rent per year is:

$£20,000 \times [50 - (10 - 1)] \times 2\% \times 1/10 = £1,640$

(h) **Rents are taxed under Schedule A, not Schedule D Case I**.

(i) **Capital allowances are the statutory substitute for depreciation**.

(j) The following items require no adjustment.

   (i)   **Patent fees,** which **are deductible** by statute.

(ii) **Debenture interest on a trading loan relationship,** which is **deductible** by statute.

(iii) **Discounts received, which simply affect the cost of purchases.**

(iv) **The insurance recovery for damage to stock, which simply replaces some or all of the revenue which would have been earned had the stock not been damaged.**

Marking guide	Marks
Lease amortisation	½
Depreciation	½
Loss on lorry	½
Entertaining/food gifts	2
Legal fees	1
Fines/penalties	1
Courses	½
Windows/routine repairs	2
Bad debts	2
Lease premium	2
Rents	½
CAs	½
Patent fees	½
Debenture interest	½
Discounts	½
Insurance recovery	½
	15

4   SCHEDULE D ADJUSTMENTS

Pass marks. It was important to answer this question by giving reasons for the adjustments you made and quoting case law where appropriate.

(a)

	£	Notes	£
Profits per accounts			290,000
Add:			
Director's salary	24,000	(ii)	
Damages	12,000	(iii)	
Repairs	12,000	(iv)	
Employee loans w/o	2,000	(v)	
Goods sold abroad	40,000	(viii)	
			90,000
Deduct:			
Decrease in general bad debt provision	3,000	(vi)	
Insurance recoveries	14,000	(ix)	
			(17,000)
			363,000

Notes

(i) **The costs of seconding employees to charities are deductible,** so no adjustment needs to be made in respect of the £22,000 paid to the director seconded to Oxfam.

(ii) **The salary paid to a director seconded to a group company** was not paid wholly and exclusively for the purpose of the company's trade so it is **not deductible** and an adjustment is needed.

(iii) **In *Strong and Co v Woodifield 1906* damages paid were held to be non-deductible because they were too remote from the trade.** In this case disallow the net costs after insurance recoveries.

(iv) **The cost of getting the office ready for use is non-deductible capital expenditure** (*Law Shipping Co Ltd v CIR 1923*).

(v) **Employee loans are not made for the purposes of the company's trade so these are non-deductible.**

(vi) **A decrease in the general bad debt provision is not taxable** so an adjustment must be made to the accounts figure. No adjustments are required in respect of specific provisions for bad debts, or in respect of bad debts written off.

(vii) **Redundancy payments in a continuing trade are deductible provided they are paid wholly and exclusively for trade purposes.**

(viii) **The company must make a transfer pricing adjustment to adjust the price of goods sold abroad to their market value.**

(ix) **Insurance recoveries in respect of the let properties are taxable under Schedule A.** This means that you need to make an adjustment to ensure the recoveries are not also included in the Schedule D profits.

(x) **Insurance recoveries in respect of repairs to the general office are taxable under Schedule D so no adjustment is needed.**

Marking guide

	Marks
Calculation	2
Secondment to charity	1
Secondment to subsidiary	1
Damages to customer	1
Repairs to new offices	1
Bad debts	3
Redundancy payments	1
Transfer pricing	2
Insurance recovery re let properties	2
Insurance re offices	1
	15

5   PREPARATION QUESTION: CORPORATION TAX COMPUTATION

Pass marks. This was a straightforward corporation tax computation, but you had to think carefully about the point of part (b). Not only has the disposal put the company into the small companies marginal rate band; it was also very close to the end of the period.

(a) **Corporation tax computation for the accounting period**

	£	£
Schedule D Case I		245,000
Schedule A		15,000
Schedule D Case III		4,000
Capital gains £(35,000 + 7,000)	42,000	
Less losses brought forward	(8,000)	
		34,000
		298,000
Less charges		(7,000)
PCTCT		291,000
Dividends plus tax credits		15,000
Profits for small companies rate purposes		306,000

£

Corporation tax £291,000 × 30%   87,300

Less small companies' marginal relief £(1,500,000 − 306,000) × $\dfrac{291,000}{306,000}$ × 11/400   (31,225)

Mainstream corporation tax   56,075

(b) The disposal on 28 March 2003 increased the 'profits' for small companies rate purposes from £299,000 to £306,000, thus leading to the application of the full rate less marginal relief. If the disposal had not been made, the mainstream corporation tax would have been only £284,000 × 19% = £53,960, a saving of £2,115. It might be that had the disposal taken place in the next accounting period, starting only four days later, the gain would only have been taxed at 19% (assuming no rate changes), giving rise to tax of £1,330. Thus the company might have been able to save tax of £2,115 − £1,330 = £785 (and this ignores the benefit of an extra month's indexation allowance). Payment of tax on the gain would also have been deferred for a further 12 months.

6   PREPARATION QUESTION: LONG PERIOD OF ACCOUNT

> **Pass marks**. A long period of account must be split into two accounting periods. The first accounting period is always twelve months long. The rest of the period of account forms the second accounting period.

Corporation tax computations

	Accounting periods		
	12m to 31.3.01 £	12m to 31.3.02 £	6m to 30.9.02 £
Adjusted trading profits (p/e 30.9.02 12:6)	148,000	318,600	159,300
Less capital allowances (W1)	(65,250)	(81,971)	(44,459)
Schedule D Case I	82,750	236,629	114,841
Schedule D Case III	18,000	15,041	5,459
Chargeable gains	108,000	0	176,250
	208,750	251,670	296,550
Less charges paid	(3,750)	(3,750)	(1,500)
Profits chargeable to corporation tax	205,000	247,920	295,050
Dividends plus tax credits ($^{100}/_{90}$)	876	1,776	8,650
Profits for small companies rate purposes	205,876	249,696	303,700

	£	£	£
Corporation tax			
FY 2000 £205,000 × 20%	41,000		
FY 2001 £247,920 × 20%		49,584	
FY 2002 £295,050 × 30%			88,515
Less small companies marginal relief			
FY 2002 £(750,000 − 303,700) × $\dfrac{295,050}{303,700}$ × 11/400			(11,924)
Mainstream corporation tax	41,000	49,584	76,591
Due date	1.1.02	1.1.03	1.7.03

Note. As the company does not pay corporation tax at the full rate, payment of the tax is due nine months after the end of the accounting period rather than in quarterly instalments.

Workings

1   **Capital allowances**

	FYA £	Pool £	Expensive car £	Allowances £
Pool b/f		213,000		
12 months to 31.3.01				
Additions		36,000	16,500	
		249,000	16,500	
WDA at 25%		(62,250)	(3,000)	65,250
		186,750	13,500	
12 months to 31.3.02				
Additions		7,800		
Disposals		(70,000)		
		124,550	13,500	
WDA at 25%		(31,138)	(3,000)	34,138
		93,412	10,500	
Additions	119,583			
FYA at 40%	(47,833)			47,833
		71,750		81,971
6 months to 30.9.02				
Disposals		(3,994)		
		161,168	10,500	
WDA at 25% × 6/12		(20,146)	(1,313)	21,459
Additions	23,000			
FYA at 100%	(23,000)			23,000
		141,022	9,187	44,459

7   **UNUSUAL URNS LTD**

> **Pass marks.** The first consideration when relieving losses is the rate at which relief will be obtained. Cash flow is a secondary consideration.

(a)   Corporation tax computation

	£
Trading profits	900,000
Less: capital allowances (W1)	(210,750)
industrial buildings allowances (W2)	(3,920)
Schedule D Case I	685,330
Schedule D Case III (£5,000 + £40,000)	45,000
	730,330
Less charge on income paid (gift aid)	(20,000)
Profits chargeable to corporation tax	710,330

	£
FY01	
£710,330 × 30% × 2/12	35,517
Less: small companies' marginal relief 1/40 (1,500,000 − 710,330) × 2/12	(3,290)
FY02	
£710,330 × 30% × 10/12	177,583
Less: small companies' marginal relief 11/400 (1,500,000 − 710,330) × 10/12	(18,097)
Mainstream corporation tax payable	191,713

As Unusual Urns Ltd is not a 'large' company, the mainstream corporation tax of £191,713 is all due for payment on 1 November 2003.

(b) The loss of £150,000 sustained in the period ended 31.1.02 could be:

   (i)   carried back under s 393A ICTA 1988 to set against the profits before charges arising in the year to 31.7.01;

   (ii) carried forward to set against Schedule D Case I trading profits arising in the year to 31.1.03.

If the loss is carried forward it will all save tax at the marginal rate of 32.75% in the year to 31.1.03. There will be no unrelieved charges as a result of the loss relief.

If the loss is carried back tax will be saved only at the small companies rate of 20%. Again, there will be no unrelieved charges as a result of the loss relief.

Whichever option is chosen, the gift aid donation in 6 months to 31.1.02 will be unrelieved.

Despite the cash flow disadvantage of not reliving losses until later, it is recommended that the losses are carried forward as this saves more tax.

Workings

1   *Capital allowances*

	FYA £	Pool £	Short life asset £	Expensive car (1) £	Expensive car (2) £	Allowances £
TWDV b/f		223,000	2,500	16,000		
Additions		60,000			35,000	
Disposals		(60,000)	(500)	(18,000)		
		223,000	2,000	(2,000)	35,000	
WDA @ 25%/ (restricted)		(55,750)			(3,000)	58,750
Balancing allowance /charge			(2,000)	2,000		-
Additions	380,000					
FYA @ 40%	(152,000)					152,000
		228,000				210,750
		395,250			32,000	

Note. The company is a medium sized enterprise for capital allowance purposes, so FYAs are due at 40%.

2   *Industrial buildings allowances*

Following the extension of the offices the total expenditure on the administration offices was £40,000. This will not qualify for IBAs in the accounting period to 31.1.03 as it exceeds 25% of the total expenditure potentially qualifying for IBAs.

Expenditure qualifying for IBAs

	£
Levelling land	2,000
Factory	90,000
Architect's fees	6,000
	98,000

IBAs 4% × £98,000 = £3,920

Marking Guide			Marks
(a)	– loan interest		1
	– bank interest		1
	– gift aid donation		1
	Capital allowances		
	– plant and machinery		1
	– sales		1
	– additions		1
	– WDAs		1
	– balancing charge		1
	– balancing allowance		1
	– FYA		2
	– industrial buildings		
	– 1998 costs		1
	– levelling land		1
	– factory		1
	– architect's fees		1
	– exclusion of administration offices		2
	– WDA		1
	Calculation of corporation tax		
	– full rate		1
	– small companies' marginal relief		1
	Payment date		2
			22
(b)	(i)	Carry back (s 393A(1))	1
		Carry forward (s 393(1))	1
	(ii)	Deciding factor	2
		Marginal rate CAP to 31.7.01	1
		Marginal rate CAP to 31.1.03	1
		Charges	1
			7
			29

8 UNFORSEEN ULTRASONICS LTD

> **Pass marks**. You had to spot that the managing director's old car was cheap enough to have been pooled, even though his new car had to be kept out of that pool because it cost over £12,000.

Unforseen Ultrasonics Limited
Corporation tax computation

	£
Trading profit	2,300,000
Less capital allowances (W1)	(93,650)
Schedule D Case I	2,206,350
Less loss brought forward (no balance to c/f)	(600,000)
	1,606,350
Schedule D Case III £(1,500 + 80,000)	81,500
Chargeable gains (W2)	0
	1,687,850
Less charges	(5,000)
Profits chargeable to corporation tax	1,682,850

Corporation tax	£
FY01	
£1,682,850 × 30% × 3/12	126,214
FY02	
£1,682,850 × 30% × 9/12	378,641
Mainstream corporation tax	504,855

Note. Companies pay gift aid donations gross.

As Unforseen Ultrasonics Ltd pays corporation tax at the full rate, its corporation tax liability for the year to 31.12.02 was due for payment by quarterly instalments as follows:

Due date	*Amount due*
	£
14 July 2002	126,214
14 October 2002	126,214
14 January 2003	126,214
14 April 2003	126,213
	504,855

Workings

1   **Capital allowances**

(a)   The industrial building

The total for the original building, excluding land, is £430,000, and the office part (£70,000) is less than 25% of this, so all £430,000 initially qualifies.

The new extension (£60,000) puts the total cost of the office part up to £130,000, which is over 25% of the new total expenditure of £490,000: this means none of the expenditure on the offices will now qualify.

IBAs are £360,000 × 4% = £14,400.

(b)   Plant and machinery

	FYA	*Pool*	*Expensive car*	*Short-life asset*	*Total*
	£	£	£	£	£
WDV b/f		190,000		4,000	
Transfer		4,000		(4,000)	
		194,000			
Additions			18,000		
Disposals		(18,000)			
		176,000	18,000		
WDA @ 25%		(44,000)	(3,000)		47,000
Additions	80,625				
FYA @ 40%	(32,250)				32,250
		48,375			
					79,250
WDV c/f		180,375	15,000		

As the company is a small or medium sized enterprise, FYAs are due at 40%.

(c)   Total allowances are £(14,400 + 79,250) = £93,650.

2 **Capital gains**

	£
Proceeds	72,493
Less: cost	(27,000)
Unindexed gain	45,493
Less: indexation allowance	

$$\frac{175.2 - 106.7 \ (= 0.642) \times £27,000}{106.7}$$ (17,334)

	£
Indexed gain	28,159
Less: loss b/f	(28,159)
Chargeable gain	Nil
Loss c/f £(30,000 – 28,159)	£1,841

Marking guide

	Marks
Capital allowances	
- industrial building	3
- plant and machinery	4
Loss b/f	1
Sch D Case III	2
Gains	
- calculation	5
- loss use	1
- loss c/f	1
Charges	1
PCTCT	1
Corporation tax liability	3
Instalments of CT	2
Details	2
Balance due	2
	28

---

9 **INDUSTRIAL LTD**

Pass marks. This question is a typical example of the compulsory 30 mark question that you will be faced with in Section A of your exam. Do not allow the length of the question to overwhelm you – you should break the question down into parts as you work through it.

The amount of patent royalties charged in the accounts are deducted in arriving at the Schedule D Case I income. If you have studied tax before, note that this is a Finance Act 2002 change.

(a) *Corporation tax payable y/e 31.3.03*

	£	£
Trading profit	1,689,710	
Less: Patent royalties	(12,000)	
Less: Capital allowances		
- on Factory (W1)	(12,000)	
- on Plant and machinery (W2)	(42,110)	
Schedule D Case I		1,623,600
Schedule D Case III - BI received	12,500	
- Loan interest received	36,000	48,500
Schedule A (W3)		73,200
Capital gains (W4)		67,573
Total profits		1,812,873
Less: charges on income		
- Gift Aid paid		(1,500)
PCTCT		1,811,373

Tax

	£
£1,811,373 × 30%	543,412

Workings

1 IBA

Expenditure eligible for IBAs

	£
Levelling the land	9,200
Architects fees	24,300
Concrete floor	16,500
Factory	187,500
General offices (less than 25% of total)	62,500
	300,000
IBA @ 4% (building in use on 31.3.03)	£12,000

2 *Plant and machinery*

	FYAs £	General pool £	Expensive car (1) £	Expensive car (2) £	Allowances given £
TWDV b/f		84,600	15,400		
Addition not qualifying				17,200	
Disposal			(19,600)		
Balancing charge			4,200		(4,200)
WDA @ 25%		(21,150)		(3,000) (max)	24,150
		63,450		14,200	
Additions qualifying for FYA					
Heating system	12,800				
Fire alarm system	7,200				
Computer (N)	3,400				
Lorry	32,000				
	55,400				
	(22,160)				
Less: FYA @ 40%		33,240			22,160
TWDV c/f		96,690	-	14,200	
Allowances given					42,110

Note. The computer equipment does not qualify for 100% FYA as Industrial Ltd is not a 'small' enterprise.

3 *Schedule A*

	£	£
Premium		
Amount received	80,000	
Less: 2% × (10 − 1) × 80,000	(14,400)	
Assessable under Schedule A		65,600
Rental (3/12 × £30,400)		7,600
Schedule A profit		73,200

4 *Capital gain on sale of shares*

	£
Proceeds	223,000
Less: cost	(135,800)
Unindexed gain	87,200
Less: indexation allowance	(8,827)
Indexed gain	78,373
Less: loss b/f	(10,800)
Net gains	67,573

(b) (i)   Industrial Ltd is a 'large' company as it pays corporation tax at the full rate and did so in the previous year. Therefore it is required to make quarterly payments on account of corporation tax.

(ii) Industrial Ltd must pay its liability in four equal instalments. These are due on 14th October 2002; 14 January 2003; 14th April 2003 and 14th July 2003.

10   PREPARATION QUESTION: PLANT AND A FACTORY

> **Pass marks**. The tax benefit of capital allowances depends on the applicable rate of corporation tax, as set out in part (b). This fact may influence the timing of capital expenditure, if a company's tax rate fluctuates.
>
> As the company is a small enterprise for first year allowances purposes, 100% first year allowances are available on the computer equipment. 40% first year allowances are available on other plant. FYAs are not pro-rated in short periods.

(a) **Capital allowances**

		£	*Total* £
(i)	*Computer equipment £2,500: FYA @ 100%*		2,500
(ii)	*Cars*		
	General pool: 25% × 10/12 × £5,000	1,042	
	Expensive: allowance restricted to £3,000 × 10/12	2,500	
			3,542
(iii)	*Plant £65,842 FYA @ 40%*		26,337

Industrial building

The original owner would have received IBAs but since the building was sold less than 25 years after 5 December 1988 a balancing charge would have been applied on sale. Freddie Ltd is given WDAs on the 'residue after sale' which is, generally, the lower of proceeds or original cost. Thus allowances will be given on £7,500 (£10,000 − £2,500). The building was 14 years 9 months old when Freddie acquired it. Of the 25 years tax life, 10 years 3 months (123 months) remain. Allowances of £7,500 × 12/123 are given each full year, but only 10/123 in this first, short period. Thus: £7,500 × 10/123

			610
(iv)	*Extension to factory*		
	WDA 4% × 10/12 × £222,000		7,400
	Total allowances		40,389

(b) **The tax benefit of capital allowances**

For corporation tax purposes capital allowances are treated as a trading expense. They therefore reduce the taxable profit of the accounting period to which they relate. If Freddie Ltd makes profits exceeding £1,500,000 × 10/12 = £1,250,000, its profits will be taxed at 30%. The tax saved by virtue of the capital allowances will therefore be £40,389 × 30% = £12,117. If profits are less than £300,000 × 10/12 = £250,000 but above £50,000 × 10/12 = £41,667, the small companies rate of 19% will apply. The value of the allowances will then be £7,674. If profits are below £10,000 × 10/12 = £8,333, the starting rate of corporation tax applies and the value of allowances is then £NIL.

If profits fall between the limits of £1,250,000 and £250,000 the marginal rate of tax will be 32.75%, giving a tax saving of £13,227. If profits fall between the limits of £41,667 and £8,333, the marginal rate of tax will be 23.75% giving a tax saving of £9,592.

The cash flow benefit of the capital allowances will not be felt until the due date for payment of the mainstream corporation tax: provided the company does not pay tax at the full rate this will be 1 January 2004. If the company pays tax at the full rate it will normally have to make quarterly payments on account of its corporation tax liability.

If capital allowances create or increase a loss the benefit will be enjoyed only under the loss relief provisions. It would be beneficial to disclaim allowances so that profits were brought down to £8,333.

(c) **Expenditure on office accommodation**

Rent payable is allowable as a trading expense. **A lease premium, to the extent that it is taxable income of the landlord, will be divided into yearly deductions depending on the length of the lease. No industrial buildings allowance is given on the purchase of office accommodation except for expenditure of not more than 25% of the cost of an industrial building.** Office equipment, including certain fixtures such as carpets, does attract capital allowances as plant. Repairs are deductible expenses unless disallowed as capital expenditure.

11 UNFORGETTABLE UNITS LIMITED

> **Pass marks.** It is very important that you learn to deal with industrial buildings allowances.

Corporation tax computation

	£
Schedule D Case I (W1)	756,465
Schedule D Case III (£64,000 + £5,000)	69,000
Less: charges on income paid	(58,000)
Profits chargeable to corporation tax	767,465

Corporation tax (W4)

	£
FY 2001 and FY 2002	
£767,465 × 30%	230,240
FY 2001	
$1/40(1,500,000 - 779,965) \times \dfrac{767,465}{779,965} \times {}^{7}/_{12}$	(10,332)
FY 2002	
Less: $11/400 (1,500,000 - 779,965) \times \dfrac{767,465}{779,965} \times {}^{5}/_{12}$	(8,118)
Corporation tax payable	211,790

Workings

1   *Schedule D Case I*

		£
Profit per accounts		822,875
Add:	Gift aid donations	58,000
	Fine	10,000
Less:	Reduction in bad debt provision	(5,000)
	Debenture interest	(64,000)
	Bank interest	(5,000)
	Dividend	(11,250)
	Capital allowances (W2)	(41,500)
	Industrial buildings allowance (W3)	(7,660)
Schedule D Case I		756,465

As fines are not incurred wholly and exclusively for the purpose of the trade they are not deductible in computing Schedule D Case I profits.

2 *Capital allowances*

	FYA £	Pool £	Expensive car £	Allow- ances £
TWDV b/f		100,000		
Addition			13,000	
Disposal		(2,000)		
		98,000	13,000	
WDA @ 25%/ restricted		(24,500)	(3,000)	27,500
Additions	35,000			
FYA @ 40%	(14,000)			14,000
		21,000		41,500
		94,500	10,000	

Unforgettable Units Ltd qualifies for 40% first year allowances as it is a small or medium sized enterprise for capital allowance purposes.

3 *Industrial buildings allowance*

IBAs are due on the lower of purchase price (£250,000) and original cost (£150,000), ie on £150,000.

Tax life ends on 1.8.2021

Date of purchase is 1.1.2002

Unexpired life is therefore 19 years 7 months

Allowances due to Unforgettable Units Ltd

$$\frac{\text{Residue after sale}}{\text{Remaining tax life}} = \frac{150,000}{19\,^7\!/_{12}} = £7,660$$

4 *'Profits'*

	£
Profits chargeable to corporation tax	767,465
FII (£11,250 × 100/90)	12,500
'Profits'	779,965

As 'profits' are between the upper and lower limits for small companies' rate purposes for FY 2001 and FY 2002 small companies' marginal relief applies in both years.

Marking Guide	**Marks**
Debenture interest and bank interest	1
Charges on income	1
Profit adjustment statement -	
Gift aid	1
Legal expenses	1
Bad debts	4
Debenture interest	1
Bank interest	1
Dividend	1
Capital allowances – plant and machinery	
Additions	1
Sales	1
WDAs	1
FYA	1
Capital allowances – industrial buildings	
Allowances on cost/original purchase price	3
Remaining tax life	3
Allowances given	3
Corporation tax payable	
Calculation of 'P'	2
Marginal relief	2
	28

12   PREPARATION QUESTION: CARRYING BACK A LOSS

> **Pass marks**. It was necessary to spot that starting rate marginal relief would apply in the year to 31 March 2003. Now that the starting rate of tax is 0%, you need to think carefully before you set a loss against profits that would otherwise be taxed at 0%.

(a)

	Year ended 31 March		
	2001	*2002*	*2003*
	£	£	£
Schedule D Case I	125,000	0	50,000
Less s 393(1) loss relief	0	0	0
	125,000	0	50,000
Schedule D Case III	263,000	10,000	24,000
Chargeable gains (loss c/f)	60,360	0	0
	448,360	10,000	74,000
Less s 393A(1) current loss relief	0	(10,000)	0
	448,360	0	74,000
Less: s 393A carry back	(415,000)	0	0
Less: gift aid donation	(33,360)	0	(30,000)
Profits chargeable to corporation tax	0	0	44,000
Unrelieved gift aid donation	6,640	47,000	0

The loss carried back is £465,000 – £50,000 = £415,000. There is no remaining trading loss to carry forward.

There is no corporation tax liability for either of the first two years.

For the third year, the position is as follows.

Profits chargeable to corporation tax = £44,000.

'Profits' = £44,000 + (£3,750 × 100/90) = £48,167. As 'profits' are between the starting rate upper and lower limits of £50,000 and £10,000 respectively, starting rate marginal relief applies.

	£
Corporation tax	
£44,000 × 19%	8,360
Less: starting rate marginal relief	
$^{19}/_{400}$ (£50,000 − £48,167) × $\dfrac{44,000}{48,167}$	(80)
	8,280

The current year set off is in some ways not worth taking in this question as the company's profits **would otherwise be taxed at the starting rate of 0%**. However, if a current year set off is not made a s 393A carryback claim cannot be made. In this case carrying the loss back saves tax at 32.75%, 19% and 23.75%. The claim must be for the whole of the loss under s393A. If s 393A claims were not made the loss would have to be carried forward and based on current year profits relief would be at 23.75% in future years. However, as relief would not be available for several years, the company may still prefer to carry the loss back.

(b) The due date for payment of the £8,280 corporation tax for the year to 31 March 2003 is 1 January 2004. The filing date is 31 March 2004. **Galbraith Ltd is not required to pay its anticipated corporation tax liability in quarterly instalments as it does not pay corporation tax at the full rate.**

13 UNPLUGGED UTENSILS LTD

> **Pass marks.** It is important to work systematically through a question like this, dealing with the loss in the earliest year first.

(a)

		Year ended		5 months	Year ended	
	31.7.99	31.7.00	31.7.01	31.12.01	31.12.02	31.12.03
	£	£	£	£	£	£
Schedule D Case I	150,000	50,000	0	58,000	0	50,000
Less: s 393(1) ICTA 1988	0	0	0	0	0	(50,000)
Schedule A	4,000	0	22,000	0	20,000	0
Capital gain	0	5,000	0	0	0	0
Schedule D III	0	0	20,000	10,000	0	4,000
	154,000	55,000	42,000	68,000	20,000	4,000
Less: s 393A (W1/W2) current	0	0	(42,000)	0	(20,000)	0
	154,000	55,000	0	68,000	0	4,000
Less: s 393A c/b (W1)	0	(8,000)	0	0	0	0
(W2)	0	0	0	(68,000)	0	0
	154,000	47,000	0	0	0	4,000
Less: Non trade charges	0	(2,000)	0	0	0	(4,000)
PCTCT	154,000	45,000	0	0	0	0
CT at 20%	£30,800	£9,000				
Unrelieved non trade charges			£2,000	£2,000	£4,000	

(b)   Capital losses c/f at 1.01.04 are £1,000 (£6,000 – £5,000)

Amounts carried forward under s 393(1)(9) ICTA 1988 on 1.01.04 are:

	£
Unrelieved losses (W2)	62,000

Workings

1   **Loss y/e 31.7.01**

	£
Loss	50,000
Less: s 393A current	(42,000)
	8,000
S 393A - c/b	(8,000)
	0

2   **Loss y/e 31.12.02**

	£
Loss	200,000
Less s 393A current	(20,000)
	180,000
S 393A c/b p/e 31.12.01	(68,000)
c/f	112,000
S 393(1) y/e 31.12.03	(50,000)
c/f at 1.01.04	62,000

Marking Guide		**Marks**
(a)	CAP to 31.12.03	
	Loss b/f s393(1) £50,000	1
	CAP to 31.12.01	
	Capital loss c/f	2
	Charges on income	1
	Other income	1
	Working 1 (Loss to 31.7.01):	
	S393A current	1
	S393A c/b	1
	Working 2 (Loss to 31.12.02):	
	S393A current	1
	S393A c/b	2
	CT liabilities	2
		12
(b)	Capital losses carried forward	1
	Unrelieved trading loss c/f	2
		3
		15

14 PREPARATION QUESTION: A BUILDING AND SHARES

> **Pass marks**. Rollover relief is not automatically available on the facts given: conditions relating to trade use and the time of acquisition must be satisfied.

(a) (i) **The building**

	£
Proceeds	200,000
Less cost	(65,000)
Unindexed gain	135,000
Less indexation allowance	

$$£65,000 \times \frac{174.6 - 89.1}{89.1} = 0.960$$ (62,400)

Chargeable gain	72,600

(ii) **The Z plc shares**

	Shares	Cost £	Indexed cost £
The FA 1985 pool			
May 1982 acquisition	2,000	4,000	4,000
Indexation to April 1985:			

$$£4,000 \times \frac{94.8 - 81.6}{81.6} = 0.162$$

			648
			4,648
Indexed rise to March 1986:			

$$£4,648 \times \frac{96.7 - 94.8}{94.8} = 0.02$$

			93
March 1986 acquisition	2,000	5,000	5,000
	4,000	9,000	9,741
Indexed rise to July 2002:			

$$£9,741 \times \frac{174.8 - 96.7}{96.7} = 0.808$$

			7,871
			17,612
July 2002 disposal	(4,000)	(9,000)	(17,612)
	0	0	0

	£
Sale proceeds	22,000
Less cost	(9,000)
	13,000
Less indexation allowance £(17,612 – 9,000)	(8,612)
Indexed gain	4,388

Total chargeable gains for the year are £72,600 + £4,388 = £76,988.

Corporation tax payable thereon is £76,988 × 30% = £23,096.

(b) **If the non-industrial building was occupied and used for trading purposes and the sale proceeds are reinvested in another building (or other qualifying asset) for use in the company's trade, within 12 months before or 36 months after the disposal, capital gains rollover relief will be available.**

If the new qualifying building costs £225,000, full rollover relief will be available with the chargeable gain arising on the disposal (£72,600) being deducted from the acquisition cost of the new building, to give the revised base cost of that asset.

When not all of the sale proceeds of a qualifying asset are reinvested, the gain which becomes immediately chargeable is the lower of:

(i)   the gain on disposal of the old asset; and

(ii)   the proceeds not reinvested in the new asset.

Thus, if the new building costs £175,000, a gain of £25,000 becomes chargeable immediately, with the balance of £72,600 – £25,000 = £47,600 being rolled over.

15   ABC LTD

> **Passmarks.** The question emphasised that you were not required to calculate the total corporation tax payable by ABC Ltd. You would not have gained any marks for doing so.

(a)   **Gain on disposal of land in May 1995**

		£
Sale proceeds in May 1995		140,000
Less cost		(80,000)
		660,000
Less: Indexation allowance = 0.409 × £80,000		(32,720)
		27,280
Gain rolled over		(17,280)
Proceeds retained (£140,000 – £130,000)		10,000

Sale of land

	£	£
Sale proceeds		700,000
Less : Cost	130,000	
Less: gain rolled	(17,280)	
		(112,720)
		587,280
Less: Indexation allowance = 0.149 × £112,720		
		(16,795)
Chargeable gain		570,485

DEF Ltd shares

	£
Proceeds	700,000
Less cost	(40,000)
	660,000
Less: indexation allowance 0.529 × £40,000	
	(21,160)
	638,840

(b)   **Funds for loan repayment**

As ABC Ltd and DEF Ltd are associated companies, the small companies rate thresholds are divided by two, giving upper and lower limits for small companies rate purposes of £750,000 and £150,000 respectively. Because of the other chargeable income of £150,000 for the year ended 31 March 2003, the chargeable gains will bear corporation tax at the marginal rates of 32.75% on £600,000 and 30% on any excess.

	Plot of land	DEF Ltd Shares
	£	£
Proceeds	700,000	700,000
Corporation tax at marginal rate of 32.75%	(186,834)	(196,500)
Corporation tax at marginal rate of 30%		(11,652)
Net sale proceeds	513,166	491,848

The directors need approximately £512,000 in order to repay the loan, so only the sale of the land generates sufficient net sale proceeds to repay the loan.

They should be advised to sell the plot of land rather then the shares, since this generates more net cash after taking into account the corporation tax that must be paid on the chargeable gain.

In addition, if either ABC Ltd or DEF Ltd buys further capital assets qualifying for rollover relief within the next three years, the gain arising on the sale of the land can once more be deferred through rollover relief.

Marking guide

			Marks
(a)	Disposal of land 1995		3
	Sale of land -	Proceeds less cost	1
		Rollover gain	1
		IA	1
		Gain	1
	DEF shares		3
			10
(b)	Small companies limits		1
	Land sale tax		2
	Shares sale tax		2
			5
			15

---

16   PREPARATION QUESTION: FOREIGN TAX

Pass marks. The four associated companies reduce Mumbo Ltd's upper limit for small companies' marginal relief purposes to £300,000 and this makes marginal relief unavailable. This greatly simplifies the calculation.

Mumbo Ltd
Corporation tax computation

	£	£
Schedule D Case I		550,000
Schedule D Case V		
Z Inc: £36,000 × 100/72	50,000	
X SA: £38,000 × 100/95	40,000	
		90,000
		640,000
Less charge paid		(60,000)
Profits chargeable to corporation tax		580,000

	£
Corporation tax £580,000 × 30%	174,000
Less double taxation relief (W)	(16,000)
Mainstream corporation tax	158,000

Working: double taxation relief

Neither foreign tax rate exceeds the UK corporation tax rate, and the charges can all be set against UK profits. Full relief is therefore available for foreign tax.

	Profits £	Charges £	Net profits £	Corporation tax at 30% £	DTR £
UK	550,000	60,000	490,000	147,000	0
Z Inc	50,000	0	50,000	15,000	14,000
X SA	40,000	0	40,000	12,000	2,000
Total	640,000	60,000	580,000	174,000	16,000

17 B AND W LTD

> **Pass marks**. The set off of DTR must be made on a source by source basis.

Mainstream corporation tax

	B Ltd £	W Ltd £
Schedule D Case I	296,000	6,000
Capital gains	30,000	0
Schedule D Case V ($\times$ 100/80)	2,000	0
Schedule D Case III	8,000	0
Less charge on income	(18,000)	0
PCTCT	318,000	6,000
FII	32,000	0
'Profits'	350,000	6,000

B Ltd

	FY01(2/12) £	FY02(10/12) £
Profits	58,333	291,667
PCTCT	53,000	265,000
Lower limit for small companies rate	25,000	125,000
Upper limit for small companies rate	125,000	625,000

Small companies' marginal relief applies in both years.

	£
FY 01	
£53,000 $\times$ 30%	15,900
Less: $\frac{1}{40}(125,000 - 58,333) \times \frac{53,000}{58,333}$	(1,514)
FY 02	
£265,000 $\times$ 30%	79,500
Less: $\frac{11}{400}(625,000 - 291,667) \times \frac{265,000}{291,667}$	(8,329)
	85,557
Less DTR (W1)	(400)
Mainstream corporation tax	85,157

W Ltd

CT   £

FY 2001

£6,000 × 20% × 2/12   200

Less: 1/40 (25,000 – 6,000) × 2/12   (79)

                                                                              121

FY 2002

£6,000 × 19% × 10/12   950

Less: starting rate marginal relief (W2)

    19/400 (£25,000 – £6,000) × 10/12   (752)

Mainstream corporation tax   319

Workings

1 **Double tax relief**

	UK profits £	Schedule D Case V £	Total £
Profits	334,000	2,000	336,000
Less: charges	(18,000)	–	(18,000)
	316,000	2,000	318,000

$$CT\ \frac{85,557}{318,000} = 26.90471\%$$

	85,019	538	85,557
Less: DTR lower of			
(i) UK tax (£538)			
(ii) Overseas tax (£400)		(400)	(400)
	85,019	138	85,157

2 **CT**

The upper and lower limits for starting rate purposes are £25,000 and £5,000 respectively so starting rate marginal relief applies.

Marking guide

			Marks
B Ltd -	Sch DI		½
	Capital gain		½
	Sch DV		1
	Sch DIII		½
	Charge		½
	FII		½
W Ltd -	Sch DI/PCTCT		½
B Ltd -	FY01 tax		2
	FY02 tax		2
DTR -	UK profits		1
	Sch DV		1
	Rate of CT		1
	DTR set off		1
W Ltd -	CT		3
			15

BPP PROFESSIONAL EDUCATION

18 X LTD

> **Pass marks.** It was important to read the question with care. For instance, you should have taken care not to readjust the profit figure which was already given as adjusted.

(a) **Capital allowances**

	FYA £	Pool £	Expensive car £	Total allowances £
WDV b/f		102,000	18,000	
WDA @ 25%		(25,500)	(3,000) (max)	28,500
		76,500	15,000	
Additions	12,000			
	23,750			
	35,750			
Less: FYA @ 40%	(14,300)			14,300
	21,450			42,800
WDV c/f		97,950	15,000	

(b) **Calculation of profits chargeable to CT**

	£
Adjusted profit	220,000
Less: Capital allowances	(42,800)
Schedule D Case I	177,200
Schedule D Case III	40,000
Schedule D Case V	4,000
Schedule A	nil
	221,200
Less: Charges on income:	
Gift aid	(8,000)
	213,200
Less: Schedule A loss relief	(17,000)
PCTCT	196,200
FII	15,000
	211,200

For the purposes of determining the small companies rate limits, both Z Ltd and Y Ltd need to be treated as associated companies, since they are both deemed to have been associated for the whole period. The limits are therefore £1,500,000/3 = £500,000 and £300,000/3 = £100,000.

MCT payable by X Ltd

	£
Tax payable at 30%	58,860
Less: small companies' marginal relief	
$£(500,000 - 211,200) \times \dfrac{196,200}{211,200} \times 11/400$	(7,378)
	51,482
Less: DTR re foreign dividend lower of:	
(i) UK tax: $\dfrac{4,000}{196,200} \times £51,482 = £1,050$	
(ii) Foreign tax: $£4,000 \times 25\% = £1,000$	
	(1,000)
MCT payable	50,482

£50,482 is due for payment on 1 February 2004.

X Ltd does not have to pay its CT in quarterly instalments because it does not pay corporation tax at the full rate.

Marking guide

			Marks
(a)	FYA		1
	WDAs		1
	Allowances		<u>1</u>
			3
(b)	Sch D Case I		1
	Sch D Case III		1
	Sch D Case V		1
	Gift aid		1
	Sch A loss		1
	FII		1
	CT calculation		2
	DTR		2
	Due date		<u>2</u>
			<u>12</u>
			<u>15</u>

19 PREPARATION QUESTION: GROUP RELIEF

Pass marks. You are asked to use group relief in the most efficient manner. This means giving it first to companies in the small companies' marginal relief band, then to companies paying tax at the full rate and then to companies in the starting rate marginal relief band. You must recognise that T Ltd is an associated company, being under common control with the P Ltd group.

(a) There are six associated companies, so the lower and upper limits for small companies' rate purposes are £50,000 and £250,000 respectively. The upper and lower limits for starting rate purposes are £8,333 and £1,667 respectively.

S Ltd and T Ltd are outside the P Ltd group for group relief purposes. P Ltd's loss should be surrendered first to Q Ltd, to bring its taxable profits down to £50,000, then to R Ltd to bring its taxable profits down to £50,000 and finally to M Ltd.

Note that there is no point in P Ltd setting off any of its own loss as P Ltd is not subject to tax on its PCTCT.

	M Ltd £	P Ltd £	Q Ltd £	R Ltd £	S Ltd £	T Ltd £
Schedule D Case I	10,000	0	64,000	260,000	0	70,000
Schedule A	0	6,000	4,000	0	0	0
	10,000	6,000	68,000	260,000	0	70,000
Less charges	(4,000)	(4,500)	(2,000)	(5,000)	0	0
	6,000	1,500	66,000	255,000	0	70,000
Less group relief	(2,000)	0	(16,000)	(205,000)	0	0
PCTCT	4,000	1,500	50,000	50,000	0	70,000
Corporation tax: at 0%		0				
at 19%	760		9,500	9,500	0	
at 30%						21,000

Less starting rate marginal relief
$19/400 \times £(8,333 - 4,000)$ (206)

Less: small companies
rate marginal relief
$11/400 \ (£250,000-70,000)$ (4,950)

| MCT payable | 554 | 0 | 9,500 | 9,500 | 0 | 16,050 |

(b) If P Ltd were to acquire another 8% of the share capital of S Ltd, bringing the total holding to 75%, S Ltd's losses could be surrendered to P Ltd, Q Ltd, R Ltd or M Ltd.

20 PREPARATION QUESTION: CORRESPONDING ACCOUNTING PERIODS

> **Pass marks**. The maximum group relief in each corresponding period is the lower of the time-apportioned profits and the time-apportioned losses.

Harry Ltd

	12 months to 31.12.01	9 months to 30.9.02
	£	£
Schedule D Case I	25,000	0
Schedule A	3,000	4,000
	28,000	4,000
Less charges on income	(2,000)	(2,000)
Profits chargeable to corporation tax	26,000	2,000
Corporation tax payable		
£26,000 × 20% × 3/12	1,300	
£26,000 × 20% × 9/12	3,900	
£2,000 × 10% × 3/9		67
£2,000 × 0% × 6/9		0
Mainstream corporation tax	5,200	67

Sid Ltd

	12 months to 31.3.02	12 months to 31.3.03
	£	£
Schedule D Case I	52,000	250,000
Schedule D Case III	8,000	10,000
	60,000	260,000
Less charges on income	(5,000)	(5,000)
	55,000	255,000
Less group relief (W)	(13,750)	(30,000)
Profits chargeable to corporation tax	41,250	225,000

Corporation tax payable

	£	£
FY 2001		
£41,250 × 20%	8,250	
FY 2002		
£225,000 × 30%		67,500
Less small companies marginal relief		
Less 11/400 × (750,000 – 225,000)		(14,438)
Mainstream corporation tax	8,250	53,062

Working: group relief

	£
Loss in 9 month accounting period to 30.9.02	45,000

Less surrender to Sid Ltd (y/e 31.3.02), restricted to lower of:

			£
(i)	£45,000 × 3/9 =	£15,000	
(ii)	£55,000 × 3/12 =	£13,750	(13,750)
			31,250

Less surrender to Sid Ltd (y/e 31.3.03), restricted to lower of:

			£
(i)	£45,000 × 6/9 =	£30,000	(30,000)
(ii)	£255,000 × 6/12 =	£127,500	
Unrelieved loss carried forward			1,250

21   **A LTD**

> **Pass marks**. B Ltd's loss could be set only against the available profits of the corresponding accounting period.

Corporation Tax computation

	£	£
Schedule D Case I		42,000
Schedule A		13,000
Schedule D Case III		
Bank interest accrued	5,000	
Loan interest accrued	8,000	
		13,000
		68,000
Less: charges on income:		
Gift aid		(17,000)
		51,000
Less: group relief (W1)		(34,000)
PCTCT		17,000
Add: Franked Investment Income		1,000
'Profits'		18,000

	£
Corporation tax	
FY2002	
£17,000 × 19%	3,230
Less: starting rate marginal relief	
$19/400 \, (£18{,}750 - 18{,}000) \times \dfrac{17{,}000}{18{,}000}$	(34)
Mainstream corporation tax	3,196

£3,196 must be paid by 1 October 2003.

The corporation tax return for the period must be filed by 31.12.03.

Notes

It is assumed that the loan interest and the bank interest arose on non-trading loans and is therefore taxable under Schedule D Case III.

Workings

1   B Ltd joined the group with A Ltd on 1.7.02 so for A Ltd's profit making accounting period to 31.12.02 there are 6 months in common with B Ltd's loss making period.

   Thus

A Ltd	6/9 × £51,000	= £34,000
B Ltd	6/12 × (£130,000)	= £65,000

   Maximum group relief available is lower of two, ie £34,000.

2   The 9 months to 31.12.02 falls into FY2002.

   'Profits' are between the starting rate upper and lower limits of £50,000 × 9/12 ÷ 2 = £18,750 and £10,000 × 9/12 ÷ 2 = £3,750, so the starting rate marginal relief applies.

Marking guide

	Marks
Sch DI	½
Sch A	½
Sch DIII	2
Charges on income	1
Group relief	5
FII	1
CT calculation	3
Due dates	2
	15

22 APPLE LTD

Pass marks. The marginal rate of tax of 32.75% is an effective tax rate only. It is never actually used in working out corporation tax.

(a) Group relief is available within a 75% group. This is one where one company is a 75% subsidiary of another company or both are 75% subsidiaries of a third company. The holding company must have at least 75% of the ordinary share capital of the subsidiary; a right to at least 75% of the distributable income of the subsidiary; and the right to at least 75% of the net assets of the subsidiary were it to be wound up.

Two companies are in a group only if there is a 75% effective interest eg if Company A holds 90% of Company B which holds 90% of Company C, all three companies are in a group because 90% × 90% = 81%.

(b) Group relief should be allocated to the company with the highest marginal rate of tax. This is Cherry Ltd and Apple Ltd to the extent that profits exceed £100,000 since the small companies rate lower limit is £300,000 ÷ 3 = £100,000. Such profits are taxed at the marginal rate of 32.75%. Then, the remainder of the loss should be set against the profits of Banana Ltd which bears tax at 30%. The capital loss cannot be group relieved.

(c) Rollover relief for part of Apple Ltd's gain can be claimed in respect of the investment by Cherry Ltd. The excess of amount of proceeds over the amount invested remains in charge ie £(418,000 – 290,000) = £128,000.

An election should be made so that the asset disposed of at a loss by Banana Ltd is treated as having been disposed of by Apple Ltd. Apple Ltd will then be able to offset the loss of £8,000 against the gain of £128,000, leaving £120,000 chargeable.

Apple Ltd should then make a current year loss relief claim to bring its profits down to £100,000.

	Apple Ltd £	Banana Ltd £	Cherry Ltd £
Schedule DI	-	650,000	130,000
Net Capital gain	120,000	-	-
	120,000	650,000	130,000
Less: s 393A(1)	(20,000)		
group relief		(75,000)	(30,000)
PCTCT	100,000	575,000	100,000
Tax @ 19%	19,000		19,000
Tax @ 30%		172,500	

Note that the SCR upper limit is £1,500,000 ÷ 3 = £500,000.

23   ALPHABETIC LTD

> **Pass marks.** This question includes self assessment and the payment of corporation tax by quarterly instalments. These areas are extremely topical.

(a)   Alphabetic Ltd is a 'large' company and as such should have paid its corporation tax liability for the year to 30 September 2002 in four quarterly instalments. The underpayments were:

Due date	Amount Due	Underpaid
	£	£
14.4.02	200,000	44,000
14.7.02	200,000	44,000
14.10.02	200,000	44,000
14.1.03	200,000	44,000

Interest will run on each of the amounts of £44,000 underpaid from the due date until the date of payment, 1 July 2003.

(b)   **If a company has not received a return it must notify the Inland Revenue of its liability to corporation tax with 12 months of the end of its accounting period.**

The maximum penalty for not taking such action is 100% of the corporation tax unpaid twelve months after the end of the accounting period.

(c)   (i)   **Fixed rate penalties**

(1)   **Where the return is up to 3 months late - £100**

(2)   **Where the return is more than 3 months late - £200**

(3)   **Where the return is the third consecutive one to be filed late the above penalties are increased to £500 and £1,000 respectively.**

(ii)   **A tax geared penalty is triggered in addition to the fixed penalties if a return is more than six months late. The penalty is 10% of any tax unpaid six months after the return was due if the total delay is up to 12 months, but 20% of that tax if the return is over 12 months late.**

(d)   **Companies that become large during an accounting period will not have to pay their corporation tax for that period by instalments if:**

(i)   **their taxable profits for the period do not exceed £10 million** (reduced if there are associated companies); and

(ii)   **they were not a large company in the previous period**

A 'large company' is one that pays corporation tax at the full rate.

Also, there is a de minimis limit in that any company whose liability does not exceed £10,000 need not pay by instalments.

Marking guide

			Marks
(a)	Instalments required/paid		1
	Amount of instalments and underpayments		1
	Interest position		2
			4
(b)	Notify Inland Revenue		1
	Penalty		1
			2
(c) (i)	Fixed rate	- up to 3 months	1
		- more than 3 months	1
		- additional amounts	2
			4
(ii)	Tax geared	- when applicable	1
		- amounts	2
			3
(d) (i)	Companies becoming large		1
(ii)	De minimis limit		1
			2
			15

24 PREPARATION QUESTION: COMPUTING VAT DUE

Pass marks. VAT is due on the discounted amount whether or not the settlement discount is taken up. Bad debt relief is available if at least six months have elapsed since the payment of a debt was due.

	£	£
Output VAT		
£(210,000 - 20,000) × 17.5%		33,250
£20,000 × 0.95 × 17.5%		3,325
		36,575
Input VAT		
£130,000 × 17.5%	22,750	
Bad debt relief £4,000 × 17.5%	700	
		(23,450)
VAT due		13,125

25 NEWCOMER LTD, ONGOING LTD AND AU REVOIR LTD

Pass marks.

1   Where a discount is offered for prompt payment, VAT is chargeable on the net amount, regardless of whether the discount is taken up.

2   VAT on business entertaining is not recoverable where the cost of the entertaining is not a deductible Schedule D Case I expense.

3   Bad debt relief is only available for debts over six months old (measured from when the payment is due).

4   VAT incurred on the purchase of a car not used wholly for business purposes is not recoverable.

(a) The registration threshold is £55,000 (from 25.4.02) during any 12 month consecutive period.

This is exceeded in January 2003:

		£
2002	October	9,500
	November	14,200
	December	21,400
2003	January	12,300
		57,400

Therefore, Newcomer Ltd must register within 30 days of the end of the period ie by 2 March 2003.

Newcomer Ltd will be registered from 1 March 2003 or an earlier date agreed between the company and Customs & Excise.

(b)

	£	£
Output tax		
£120,000 × 95% = 114,000 × 17.5% (note 1)		19,950
Input tax		
£(35,640 – 480) = 35,160 × 17.5% (note 2)	6,153	
£2,000 × 17.5% (note 3)	350	
£21,150 × 7/47 (note 4)	3,150	(9,653)
VAT payable		10,297

(c) A person is eligible for voluntary deregistration if Customs and Excise are satisfied that the rate of his taxable supplies (net of VAT) in the following one year period will not exceed £53,000 (from 25.4.02). However, voluntary deregistration will not be allowed if the reasons for the expected fall in value of taxable supplies is the cessation of taxable supplies or the suspension of taxable supplies for a period of 30 days or more in that following year. HM Customs & Excise will cancel a person's registration from the date the request is made or an agreed later date.

26 SELF ASSESSMENT FOR INDIVIDUALS

> **Pass marks**. It was important to confine your answer to the points asked for in the question.

(a) (i) **The later of 30 September following the tax year to which the return relates and 2 months after the notice to file the return was issued.**

(ii) **The later of 31 January following the tax year to which the return relates and 3 months after notice to file the return was issued.**

(b) (i) The normal payment dates for Schedule D Case I and II income tax are:

- **31 January in the tax year for the first payment on account,** ie 31.1.03
- **31 July following the tax year for the second payment on account,** ie 31.7.03
- **31 January following the tax year for the final payment,** ie 31.1.04

(ii) **Each of the payments on account is normally equal to half of the schedule D Case I or II liability for the preceding year,** (in this case 2001/02).

The **final payment is the balancing payment.** It is the difference between the tax which is finally due for 2002/03 and the payments on account which have already been made in respect of the year.

(c) **Payments on account are not required if the relevant amount falls below £500.**

Also, payments on account are not required from taxpayers who paid 80% or more of their tax liability for the previous year under PAYE or other deduction at source arrangements.

(d) (i) The **fixed penalty** for not making a tax return by the filing date (31 January following the tax year) when required to do so is initially **£100**. If the **delay is more than six months** from the filing date, and the Revenue did not apply for a daily penalty within those six months, there is a **further £100 fixed penalty**.

(ii) The total of the £100 fixed penalties is reduced to the amount of the final payment of tax, if that is less than that total. The commissioners can set aside the fixed £100 penalties if they find that the taxpayer had a reasonable excuse for his conduct.

(iii) Where the Inland Revenue are of the opinion that the fixed penalties imposed will not result in the return being submitted they may ask the Commissioners to apply further penalties of up to £60 a day until the return is submitted.

Marking guide			**Marks**	
(a)	(i)	30 September/2 months	2	
	(ii)	31 January/3 months	2	
				4
(b)	(i)	31.1.03	1	
		31.7.03	1	
		31.1.04	1	
	(ii)	Payments on account	1	
		Final payment	1	
				5
(c)		£500/80% limit	2	
(d)	(i)	No return by filing date	1	
		More than 6 months late	1	
	(ii)	Reduction penalty	1	
	(iii)	Daily penalty	1	
				4
				15

27   ENQUIRIES AND DETERMINATIONS

> **Pass marks**. Do not select a question like this unless you are sure that you can give a concise answer to all parts.

(a) **The Inland Revenue must normally give notice of an enquiry by the first anniversary of the due filing date (not the actual filing date).**

(b) **If a return is filed late, the deadline by which the Revenue must give notice of an enquiry is extended to 12 months after the 31 January, 30 April, 31 July or 31 October next following the actual date of delivery of the return or amendment.**

(c) **The three main reasons** why the Revenue commence enquiries into a return are:

(i) **random selection** of the return

(ii) **the return appears unusual**; there appears to be either an underdeclaration or income or allowances appear to have been incorrectly claimed

    (iii)   **the Revenue suspect or have been informed of irregularities** in the return

(d)   The taxpayer has **30 days from the end of an enquiry to amend his self assessment** in accordance with the Revenue's conclusions.

Alternatively, a taxpayer may **appeal to the commissioners within 30 days of the end of an enquiry** if he does not accept the Revenue's conclusions.

(e)   A determination is an assessment of the amounts liable to income tax and CGT and the amount of tax due. It is issued by the Inland Revenue where the taxpayer has not submitted a return by the due filing date. It is treated as a self assessment.

A determination must be made by the 5th anniversary of 31 January following the end of the tax year.

Marking Guide

		Marks	
(a)			1
(b)	Return filed late	1	
	12 months after end of relevant quarter	<u>4</u>	
			5
(c)	(i)	1	
	(ii)	1	
	(iii)	<u>1</u>	
			3
(d)	Accept Revenue conclusions	1	
	Appeal	<u>1</u>	
			2
(e)	IT/CGT and tax	1	
	No return	1	
	Self assessment	1	
	Time limit	<u>1</u>	
			<u>4</u>
			<u><u>15</u></u>

---

28   MADELAINE AND OTTO

> **Pass marks.** It was important to state why any additional information is needed as well as what information is required.

(a)

Additional information needed	Reasons
1 Sales Were any goods taken for own use?	The market value must be included in sales
2 Stock Were any contingency reserves included in the stock valuations?	These should be added back when calculating Schedule D Case I profits.
3 Wages and National Insurance contributions (a) Were Madelaine's NIC contributions included?	If so they should be disallowed.
(b) Were any payments made to Madelaine?	If so they should be disallowed.
(c) Were any payments made to Madelaine's family?	Payments should be reasonable for the work done. Excessive payments should be disallowed.
4 Repairs and Renewals Was any capital expenditure included?	If so it should be disallowed.
5 General expenses Were any of these of a non-trading or capital nature?	If so they will be disallowed.
6 Bad debts Were there any specific or general provisions made?	Only specific provisions are allowable.
7 Interest Did the charge include any interest on overdue tax?	If so it should be disallowed.
8 Relocation expenditure Was the move to larger premises?	If so the expenditure will be disallowed.
9 Professional fees Did these include any costs in connection with capital items?	If so they will be disallowed.
10 (a) Rent and rates (b) Interest (c) Motor vehicle running costs (d) Lighting and heating (e) Professional fees (f) Subscriptions and donations Was there any private element in any of the above items?	If so, it should be disallowed.
11 Subscriptions and donations Were the donations made wholly and exclusively for trade purposes?	If not they will be disallowed.
What did the subscriptions relate to?	To be allowable they must either be wholly and exclusively for trade purposes or to a body on the Revenue approved list.

(b)

	£
1999/00 (1.6.99 – 5.4.00)	
£7,000 + 4/12 × £16,000	12,333
2000/01 (1.12.99 - 30.11.00)	16,000
2001/02 (1.12.00 - 30.11.01)	19,000

Overlap profits on commencement were £16,000 × 4/12 = £5,333. The overlap period was 4 months long.

	£
2002/03 (1.12.01 - 28.2.03)	25,000
Less: Overlap relief 3/4 × £5,333	(4,000)
Taxable	21,000

In 2002/03, 3 months worth of the overlap profits are relieved. **This ensures that only 12 months worth of profits are taxed in the year.**

Marking guide

		Marks
(a)	Goods taken for own use	$^1/_2$
	Contingency reserves	$^1/_2$
	Drawings by Madelaine/NICs	1
	Payments to family	$^1/_2$
	Repairs/renewals	$^1/_2$
	General expenses	1
	Bad debts	1
	Interest	$^1/_2$
	Relocation expenditure	1
	Professional fees	$^1/_2$
	Private usage	1
	Subscriptions and donations	1
		9
(b)	1999/00	2
	2000/01 and 2001/02	1
	2002/03	3
		6
		15

---

29   MALCOLM

Pass marks. You should not be tempted in a question like this merely to list the various loss sections. You need to make an attempt at giving your rationale for the use of the losses. Remember that you will probably get marks for your rationale even if you have not used the loss in the most efficient way.

(a) Schedule D Case I losses are:

	£	£
2001/02 (1.8.01 - 5.4.02)		
(£10,000 + 4/12 × £20,000)		(16,667)
2002/03 (1.12.01 - 30.11.02)		
Loss	20,000	
Less: Used in 2001/02	(6,667)	
		(13,333)

Each of these losses can be relieved under s 380 ICTA 1988 against STI of the year of the loss and/or the preceding year.

2001/02 loss

	2000/01 £	2001/02 £
Schedule E	8,000	5,650
Interest	3,800	3,800
STI	11,800	9,450
S 380 loss relief	(11,800)	(4,867)
	0	4,583

A s 380 ICTA 1988 claim in 2000/01 results in a waste of personal allowances. However, the claim is worthwhile as it leads to a repayment of income tax in respect of the year and the alternative is to carry the loss forward.

A s 380 ICTA 1988 claim in 2001/02 to utilise the balance of the 2001/02 loss obtains tax relief for the loss quickly and it only wastes a small amount of personal allowance.

2002/03 loss

A s380 claim in 2002/03 against interest income would not be worthwhile as it would merely waste the personal allowance. A s 380 ICTA 1988 claim in 2001/02 would also waste the personal allowance but it would allow a s 72 FA 1991 claim to be made to set the loss against the chargeable gain in 2001/02. However, this would waste the CGT annual exemption and would save only £200 (£7,900 – £7,700) × 10% = £20 of CGT.

Alternatively, if a s 380 claim was not made for the 2001/02 loss in 2000/01, the 2002/03 loss could be carried back under s 381 ICTA 1988. £11,800 of the loss would be set off in 2000/01 and the balance in 2001/02 leaving taxable income in 2001/02 of £7,917. This is clearly less beneficial than the s 380 ICTA 1988 claim for the 2001/02 loss considered above.

A better alternative is to carry the 2002/03 loss forward for relief under s385 ICTA 1998 against Schedule D Case I profits of 2003/04:

	2003/04 £
Schedule D Case I	15,000
Less: s 385 relief	(13,333)
	1,667
Building society interest	3,800
	5,467

This leaves enough income in 2003/04 to absorb the personal allowance. Income tax is saved in 2003/04 on the whole of the loss set off.

(b) **The S380 ICTA 1988 claims for the 2001/02 loss must be made by the 31 January which is nearly two years after the end of the tax year of the loss: thus by 31 January 2004.**

There is no statutory time limit by which a claim to relieve a loss under S385 ICTA 1988 must be made. **However, a claim to carry the loss of 2002/03 forward must be made by the 31 January which is nearly 5 years after the end of the year of the loss: thus by 31 January 2008.**

```
┌─────────────────────────────────────────────────────────────────────────┐
│  Marking guide                                                            │
│                                                            Marks          │
│  (a)   Calculation 2001/02 loss                             2             │
│        Calculation 2002/03 loss                             2             │
│        S 380 ICTA 1988 2000/01                              1             │
│        S 380 ICTA 1988 2001/02                              1             │
│        Order s 380 ICTA 1998 claims                         1             │
│        No s 380 ICTA 1988 2002/03                           1             │
│        Why no further s 380/s 72 or s 381 claims            2             │
│        Carry forward under s 385                            2             │
│                                                                           │
│                                                            12             │
│                                                                           │
│  (b)   S 380 time limit                                     1             │
│        S 385 time limit                                     2             │
│                                                             3             │
│                                                            15             │
└─────────────────────────────────────────────────────────────────────────┘
```

30   JACQUELINE

> **Pass marks**. It is important to realise that a terminal loss is calculated by splitting the last 12 months at 5 April. Overlap relief increases the loss arising after 5 April.

(a)   **Taxable profits**   £

1998/99
(1.5.98-5.4.99)
£5,000 + 3/12 × £8,000   7,000

1999/00
(Year to 31.12.99)   8,000

2000/01
(Year to 31.12.00)   13,000

2001/02
(Year to 31.12.01)   10,000

2002/03
(Nine months to 30.9.02)   0

(b)   **Terminal loss relief**

The terminal loss is the loss from 1 October 2001 to 30 September 2002, as follows.

1.10.01-5.4.02	£	£
1.10.01-31.12.01		
$3/12 \times £10,000$	2,500	
1.1.02-5.4.02		
$3/9 \times (£14,500)$	(4,833)	
		(2,333)
6.4.02-30.9.02		
$6/9 \times (£14,500)$		(9,667)
Overlap relief		(2,000)
Terminal loss		(14,000)

Relief is as follows.

	1998/99 £	1999/00 £	2000/01 £	2001/02 £	2002/03 £
Original profits	7,000	8,000	13,000	10,000	0
Less terminal loss	0	0	(4,000)	(10,000)	0
Final profits	7,000	8,000	9,000	0	0
Total income	7,000	8,000	9,000	0	0

Marking guide		Marks
(a)	1998/99	1
	1999/00	1
	2000/01	1
	2001/02	1
	2002/03	1
		5
(b)	Terminal loss calculation	5
	Relief - 1998/99	1
	- 1999/00	1
	- 2000/01	1
	- 2001/02	1
	- 2002/03	1
		10
		15

31   PREPARATION QUESTION: PARTNERSHIPS

Pass marks. Divide the profits of each accounting period between the partners before considering the amounts assessable in each tax year.

Each partners share of the profits is

	Total £	Clare £	Justin £	Malcolm £
1.10.99-31.1.00	26,400	8,800	17,600	0
Y/e 31.1.01	60,000	20,000	40,000	0
Y/e 31.1.02				
1.2.01-30.4.01				
(3/12 × £117,000)	29,250	9,750	19,500	0
1.5.01-31.1.02				
(9/12 × £117,000)	87,750	29,250	29,250	29,250
	117,000	39,000	48,750	29,250
Y/e 31.1.03				
1.2.02-31.12.02				
(11/12 × £108,108)	99,099	33,033	33,033	33,033
1.1.03-31.1.03				
(1/12 × £108,108)	9,009	4,505	0	4,504
	108,108	37,538	33,033	37,537

The partners will be taxed on the above profits in the following tax years.

	Clare	Justin	Malcolm
1999/00 (1.10.99-5.4.00)	£	£	Malcolm
1.10.99-31.1.00	8,800	17,600	
1.2.00-5.4.00 (2/12 × (£20,000/£40,000)	3,333	6,667	
	12,133	24,267	
2000/01 (Y/e 31.1.01)	£20,000	£40,000	
2001/02			
(Y/e 31.1.02)	£39,000	£48,750	
(1.5.01-5.4.02)			£
1.5.01-31.1.02			29,250
1.2.02-5.4.02 (2/12 × £37,537)			6,256
			35,506
2002/03			
(y/e 31.1.03)	£37,538		£37,537
(1.2.02-31.12.02)		33,033	
less: overlap relief		(6,667)	
		26,366	

Justin's overlap profits were relieved in the year he left the partnership. Clare and Malcolm have overlap profits that remain unrelieved of £3,333 and £6,256 respectively.

32   ROGER AND BRIGITTE

> **Pass marks.** First allocate the profits of each accounting period between the partners.

(a)   The profits of each partner are as follows.

		Total	Roger	Brigitte	Xavier
	£	£	£	£	£
1.10.98-30.6.99		30,000	15,000	15,000	
1.7.99 - 30.6.00		45,000	22,500	22,500	
1.7.00 - 30.6.01					
1.7.00 - 30.9.00 (3/12)	12,500		6,250	6,250	
1.10.00 - 30.6.01 (9/12)	37,500		12,500	12,500	12,500
		50,000	18,750	18,750	12,500
1.7.01 - 30.6.02		60,000	20,000	20,000	20,000

The assessable profits for the tax years are, therefore, as follows.

	Roger	Brigitte	Xavier
	£	£	£
1998/99			
(1.10.98-5.4.99)			
£15,000 × 6/9	10,000	10,000	-
1999/00			
(1.10.98 - 30.9.99)			
£15,000 + (£22,500 × 3/12)	20,625	20,625	-
2000/01			
(1.7.99 - 30.6.00)	22,500	22,500	
(1.10.00 - 5.4.01)			
£12,500 × 6/9			8,333
2001/02			
(1.7.00 – 30.6.01)	18,750	18,750	
(1.10.00 – 30.9.01)			
£12,500 + 3/12 × £20,000			17,500
2002/03			
(1.7.01 - 30.6.02)	20,000	20,000	20,000

(b) The overlap profits for both Roger and Brigitte are:

	Profits
	£
1.10.98 - 5.4.99	10,000
1.7.99 - 30.9.99	5,625
	15,625

Xavier's overlap profits are:

	£
1.10.00 - 5.4.01	8,333
1.7.01 - 30.9.01	5,000
	13,333

Marking Guide	**Marks**
Roger and Brigitte	
1998/99	2
1999/00	2
2000/01	2
2001/02	2
Xavier	
2000/01	1
2001/02	1
Combined	
2002/03	1
	11
Overlap profits	
Roger	1
Brigitte	1
Xavier	2
	4
	15

33 PARTNERSHIPS

Pass marks. This was a pilot paper question, so it should give you a really good indication of the type of question that you might meet in the exam.

Overlap profits are relieved either on a change of accounting date or on a cessation. Each partner obtains relief for their own overlap profits and their own losses.

(a) Each partner is taxed like a sole trader who runs a business which starts when he joins the partnership; finishes when he leaves the partnership; has the same periods of account as the partnership; and makes profits or losses equal to the partner's share of the partnership profits or losses.

(b)

	Total	*Anne*	*Betty*	*Chloe*
	£	£	£	£
1.1.02 – 31.12.02				
January to June	30,000	15,000	15,000	
July to December	30,000	15,000	-	15,000
Totals	60,000	30,000	15,000	15,000
1.1.03 – 31.12.03	72,000	36,000	-	36,000

Schedule DI assessments 2002/03

	Anne £	Betty £	Chloe £
Profits y/e 31.12.02	30,000		
Profits 1.1.02 – 30.6.02		15,000	
Profits 1.7.02 – 31.12.02			15,000
Profits 1.1.03 – 5.4.03			
3/12 × £36,000			9,000
	30,000	15,000	24,000
Less: overlap relief for Betty on cessation		(3,000)	
Profits assessable 2002/03	30,000	12,000	24,000

(c) (i) *Daniel*

Daniel can use his £20,000 loss:

- against total income of 2002/03 and /or of 2001/02 under s 380 ICTA 1988
- against future trading profits under s 385 ICTA 1988

(ii) *Edward*

Edward can use his £15,000 loss:

- against total income of 2002/03 and/or of 2001/02 under s 380 ICTA 1988

- if there is a terminal loss in the last 12 months of trading, against Schedule D Case II income of the tax year of cessation and the three preceding years, later years first, under s 388 ICTA 1988

(iii) *Frank*

Frank can use his loss of £5,000:

- against total income of 2002/03 and/or 2001/02 under s 380 ICTA 1988
- against total income of 1999/00, 2000/01 and 2001/02 under s 381 ICTA 1988
- against future trading profits under s 385 ICTA 1988

34 PREPARATION QUESTION: STAKEHOLDER PENSIONS

> **Pass marks.** The new stakeholder pension scheme was introduced in April 2001. It is, extremely topical and highly likely to be examined.

(a) Maximum contributions

Tax year	Age at start of tax year	Basis year	%	Maximum contribution £
2002/03	42	2002/03	20	5,000
2003/04	43	2003/04	20	16,000
2004/05	44	2003/04	20	16,000
2005/06	45	2003/04	20	16,000
2006/07	46	2003/04	25	20,000
2007/08	47	2003/04	25	20,000
2008/09	48	2003/04	25	20,000
2009/10	49	2006/07	25	18,750

Note. The % depends on age at *start of the tax year of contribution* not on age at the start of the basis year.

(b) **Personal pension contributions are paid net of basic rate tax**. This means that for a basic rate taxpayer tax relief is given at source and there is no need to take any further action.

BPP PROFESSIONAL EDUCATION

Higher rate taxpayers obtain additional relief through their personal tax computation.
The basic rate band is extended by the gross amount of the pension contribution.

35 PREPARATION QUESTION: PERSONAL COMPUTATION

> **Pass marks.** Note that the % for personal pension purposes depends on Mr Thesaurus' age at the **start** of 2002/03.

(a) **Income tax computation**

	Non-savings £	Savings (excl. dividend) £	Dividend £	Total £
Schedule D Case I	56,000			
Dividend (£900 × 100/90)			1,000	
Bank interest £1,197 × 100/80		1,496		
	56,000	1,496	1,000	
Less charges: interest on loan	(6,000)			
STI	50,000	1,496	1,000	52,496
Less personal allowance	(4,615)			
	45,385	1,496	1,000	47,881

	£
Tax on non-savings income	
£1,920 × 10%	192
£27,980 × 22%	6,156
£15,000 (extended band) × 22%	3,300
£485 × 40%	194
Tax on savings (excl. dividend) income	
£1,496 × 40%	598
Tax on dividend income	
£1,000 × 32.5%	325
Tax liability	10,765
Less tax suffered on bank interest £1,496 × 20%	(299)
tax credit on dividends £1,000 × 10%	(100)
Tax payable	10,366

(b) As 1997/98 was the basis year, the maximum gross pension premium relievable in 2002/03 is 20% × £80,000, ie £16,000.

The basic rate band is extended by the gross amount of the premium actually paid, £15,000 (£11,700 × $^{100}/_{78}$).

The interest paid on the loan to purchase a share in a partnership is eligible interest which qualifies for tax relief as a charge on income.

36 LAI CHAN

> **Pass marks.** This pilot paper question is a good example of the type of question that you might find on Section A of the exam.
>
> 1   For capital allowance purposes the WDA is restricted by the length of the basis period, but the FYA is not.
>
> 2   There is no capital allowance restriction in respect of the private use of an asset by an employee.
>
> 3   The basic rate band is extended by the gross amount of personal pension contributions made. Occupational pension contributions are, however, deducted in computing Schedule E income.

(a)   *Income tax liability 2002/03*

	£	Non-savings income £
Gross salary 9 × £3,250	29,250	
Less: pension contribution (6%)	(1,755)	
	27,495	
Car benefit (W1)	3,780	
Fuel benefit (W2)	3,150	
Beneficial loan (W3)	625	
Schedule E		35,050
Trading profit	19,900	
Less: Capital allowances (W4)	(5,860)	
Schedule D Case II profit		14,040
STI		49,090
Less: personal allowance		(4,615)
Taxable income		44,475

Tax

	£
£1,920 × 10%	192
£27,980 × 22%	6,156
£390 × 100/78 × 3 (Extended Basic Rate Band) × 22%	330
£13,075 (44,475 − 29,900 − 1,500) × 40%	5,230
Tax liability	11,908

Workings

1   *Car benefit*

	£
25% × £26,400 × 9/12 (note)	4,950
Less: contribution £130 × 9	(1,170)
	3,780

Note. The % depends on the CO_2 emissions of the car. The benefit is time apportioned as the car is available for only nine months of the year.

2   *Fuel benefit*

£4,200 × 9/12   £3,150

No reduction for partial reimbursement of private fuel cost. The benefit is time apportioned as the car was available for only nine months of the year.

3   *Beneficial loan*

Average method

$$5\% \times \frac{30,000 + 10,000}{2} \times 9/12 = \underline{£750}$$

Alternative method (strict method)

	£
£30,000 × 3/12 × 5% =	375
£10,000 × 6/12 × 5% =	250
	625

Elect for strict method

4

	FYA	General pool	Private car (60%)	Short life asset	Allowances
	£	£	£	£	£
Additions not qualifying for FYA					
- private car			14,800		
- employee car		10,400			
WDA @ 25% × 3/12		(650)			650
		9,750			
WDA @ £3,000 (restricted) × 3/12			(750) × 60%		450
			14,050		
Additions qualifying for FYA					
- recording equipment	9,300				
- recording equipment				2,600	
Less: FYA @ 40%	(3,720)			(1,040)	4,760
TWDV c/f		5,580			
Allowances		15,330	14,050	1,560	
					5,860

(b) Up to 31.12.02, PAYE will have been deducted from Lai Chan's salary. It is likely that her PAYE code was adjusted to take account of her benefits in kind. Further tax payable (or tax repayable) will be dealt with under the self-assessment system.

As Lai Chan was employed before starting in business on her own account, she is unlikely to have made any payments on account for 2002/03. Therefore, the tax on her net Schedule D Case II profit will be collected in full on 31 January 2004 under the self assessment system.

37   CLAYTON DELANEY

> **Pass marks**. In this question, you should have dealt with the adjustment of profit for the final period, then the amount assessable on cessation and finally the personal tax computation.

(a)   **The adjustment of profit for the year ended 30 June 2002**

	£	£
Net profit per accounts		8,150
Additions		
Telephone £240 × 1/5	48	
Repairs: roof £650 × 2/3	433	
Repairs: bedroom	230	
Depreciation	1,350	
Buildings insurance £600 × 2/3	400	
Lighting and heating £420 × 2/3	280	
Car expenses £1,750 × ½	875	
Bad debts: loan written off	500	
Rates: council tax	650	
Proprietor's wages	11,850	
General expenses: gifts	900	
General expenses: donation to national charity	25	
Goods for own use £600 × 100/(100 − 20)	750	
		18,291
		26,441
Deductions		
Interest received	300	
Profit on sale of shop fittings	20	
Capital allowances	3,440	
		(3,760)
Adjusted profit		22,681

Capital allowances

	Pool £	Proprietor's car (50%) £	Allowances £
Balances b/f	490	5,700	
Disposal		(4,500)	
Balancing allowance		1,200	600
Additions		9,000	
	490	9,000	
Proceeds	(400)	(3,500)	
Balancing (charge)/allowance	90	5,500	2,840
			3,440

Taxable profits

Year	Basis period	Profits £
2002/03	1.7.01 - 30.6.02	21,481

The final year's profits have been reduced by the overlap profits of £1,200.

(b) **Clayton: income tax computation**

	Non-savings	Savings (excl dividend) £	Total £
Salary £1,433.33 × 9	12,900		
Car benefit £10,000 × 19% × 9/12	1,425		
Fuel benefit £2,850 × 9/12	2,138		
Schedule E	16,463		
Schedule D Case I	21,481		
BI £395 × 100/80		494	
Annuity £50 × 8		400	
Statutory total income	37,944	894	38,838
Less personal allowance	(4,615)		
Taxable income	33,329	894	34,223

	£
Income tax on non-savings income	
£1,920 × 10%	192
£27,980 × 22%	6,156
£3,429 × 40%	1,372
Income tax on savings (excl dividend) income	
£894 × 40%	358
Tax liability	8,078
Less tax suffered on annuity £400 × 20%	(80)
Less tax suffered on BI	(99)
Tax payable (subject to tax paid under PAYE)	7,899

Note. The CO2 emissions figure of the car is 170g/km rounded down to the nearest 5. This is 5g/km above the baseline figure of 165g/km so the taxable percentage is 16% + 3% (diesel) = 19%.

Marking Guide

		Marks
(a)	Capital allowances	
	Pool	1
	Proprietor's car	2
	Disallowable items	
	Telephone	1
	Roof repairs	1
	Repairs bedroom	1
	Depreciation	1
	Insurance/light and heat	1
	Car expenses	1
	Bad debts	1
	Council tax	1
	Wages	1
	Gift	1
	Donation	1
	Goods for own use	2
	Profit on sale shop fittings/interest	1
	Overlap relief	1
	Taxable profits	_1_
		19
(b)	Salary	1
	Car benefit	3
	Fuel benefit	1
	Bank interest	1
	Annuity	_1_
		$\frac{7}{26}$

38   BRUCE

> **Pass marks.** Bruce is entitled to full allowances and the full capital gains tax annual exemption for 2002/03 even though he died part way through the year.

(a)   (i)   **Bruce's income tax liability to date of death**

	Non-savings	Savings (excl dividend)	Dividend	Total
	£	£	£	£
Retirement income	800			
Employment income	3,385			
Dividends (£10,125 × 100/90)			11,250	
Bank interest (£40 × 100/80)		50		
Total income	4,185	50	11,250	15,485
Personal allowance	(4,185)	(50)	(380)	
Taxable income	0	0	10,870	10,870

	£
Income tax on dividend income	
£10,870 at 10%	1,087
Income tax suffered:	
Tax credit on dividends	(1,087) (max)
PAYE	(380)
Tax withheld on bank interest (£50 at 20%)	(10)
Income tax repayment due	(390)

The tax credit on the dividend can only reduce the tax liability to £Nil. It cannot be repaid. However, the tax suffered on the bank interest and PAYE can be repaid.

(ii)   **Capital gains tax liability to date of death**

	£
Capital gains (no taper relief due)	32,000
Annual exemption	(7,700)
	24,300

Capital gains tax payable	£
£	
19,030 (29,900 − 10,870) × 20%	3,806
5,270 × 40%	2,108
24,300	5,914

(b)   **Capital allowances**

	FYA £	Pool £	Private use asset 50% £	Allowances £
1.6.00 – 30.4.01				
Additions			8,500	
WDA (25% × 11/12)			(1,948)	974
Additions qualifying for FYA	1,000			
FYA @ 40%	(1,000)			1,000
			6,552	1,974
1.5.01 – 30.4.02				
WDA (25%)			(1,638)	819
Additions qualifying for FYA	10,000			
FYA @ 40%	(4,000)			4,000
		6,000		
WDV c/f		6,000	4,914	4,819

Note 1. Cars do not qualify for FYAs.

Note 2. As Shiela's business is a small enterprise for capital allowance purposes, FYA are available on the cost of the computer at 100%.

Note 3. WDAs are pro-rated in the short period. FYAs are not pro-rated in short periods.

Sheila's Schedule D Case I profits are:

	£
1.6.00 – 30.4.01 (£13,500 − 1,974)	11,526
1.5.01 – 30.4.02 (£20,000 − 4,819)	15,181

Taxable profits

	£
2000/01 (1.6.00 – 5.4.01)	
(£11,526 × 10/11)	10,478
2001/02 (1.6.00 – 31.5.01)	
(£11,526 + £15,181 × 1/12)	12,791
2002/03 (1.5.01 – 30.4.02)	15,181

(c)   **Overlap profits**

'Overlap' periods are 1.6.00 – 5.4.01 and 1.5.01 – 31.5.01
'Overlap' profits are £10,478 + £1,265 = £11,743

(d) (i)   **Income tax liability**

	Non-savings
	£
Schedule D Case I	15,181
Personal allowance	(4,615)
Taxable income	10,566

Income tax on non-savings income

	£
£1,920 at 10%	192
£8,646 at 22%	1,902
	2,094

Note. **As Sheila is a basic rate tax payer, the personal pension contribution is not brought into the income tax computation. Basic rate tax relief is obtained by paying the pension contribution net of basic rate tax.**

(ii)   **Class 4 NIC liability**

	£
Profits	15,181
Lower limit	(4,615)
	10,566
£10,566 at 7% =	740

39   PREPARATION QUESTION: A COTTAGE AND SHARES

> **Pass marks.** It is important to learn the matching rules for share transactions.

(a) **The cottage**

	£	£
Proceeds £(100,000 – 800)		99,200
Less: cost 5.9.82	25,000	
expenditure 1.12.83	8,000	
		(33,000)
Unindexed gain		66,200
Less indexation allowance to April 1998		
$\dfrac{162.6 - 81.9}{81.9} = 0.985 \times £25,000$	24,625	
$\dfrac{162.6 - 86.9}{86.9} = 0.871 \times £8,000$	6,968	
		(31,593)
Gain		34,607

As this is a non-business asset owned for five years after 6.4.98 including the additional year, 85% of the gain is chargeable after taper relief, ie 85% × £34,607 = £29,416.

(b) **The disposal of shares in JVD Products plc**

Match disposals with acquisitions after 6 April 1998 on a LIFO basis:

(i)   12 August 2001 acquisition

	£
Disposal proceeds (500/4,000 × £40,000)	5,000
Less: cost	(2,000)
Chargeable gain (no taper relief)	3,000

(ii)   12 May 1999 acquisition

	£
Disposal proceeds (2,800/4,000 × £40,000)	28,000
Less: cost	(12,000)
Chargeable gain	16,000

The shares are a non-business asset so the gain after taper relief is 95% × £16,000 = £15,200. (The shares have been held for three complete years from 12.5.99.)

(iii)   1985 pool

	£
Proceeds (700/4,000 x £40,000)	7,000
Less: cost	(3,000)
Unindexed gain	4,000
Less: indexation to April 1998	
$3,000 \times \dfrac{162.6-97.8}{97.8}$	(1,988)
Indexed gain	2,012

The shares are a non-business asset so the gain on the 1985 pool after taper relief is £1,710 (85% × £2,012).

Summary

	Gains £
12.8.01 acquisition	3,000
12.5.99 acquisition	15,200
1985 pool	1,710
Total gain on shares	19,910

(c) **The tax liabilities**

	Non-savings £	Dividend £	Total £
Schedule E	8,000		
Dividends £16,200 × 100/90	-	18,000	
STI	8,000	18,000	26,000
Less personal allowance	(4,615)		
Taxable income	3,385	18,000	21,385

	£
Income tax on non savings income	
£1,920 × 10%	192
£1,465 × 22%	322
Income tax on dividend income	
£18,000 × 10%	1,800
Tax liability	2,314

Capital gains tax	£
Gain on cottage	29,416
Gain on shares	19,910
	49,326
Less annual exemption	(7,700)
Taxable gains	41,626

Capital gains tax liability	£
£8,515 (£29,900 – £21,385) × 20%	1,703
£33,111 × 40%	13,244
£41,626	14,947

40 YVONNE, SALLY AND JOANNE

> **Pass marks**. Always set losses against gains attracting the lowest rate of taper relief. The set off of losses is made before the deduction of taper relief.

(a) The sale of Yvonne's shares is initially matched with the shares bought in the next 30 days.

	£
Proceeds (1,000/5,000)	4,600
Less: cost (28.3.03)	(4,400)
Chargeable gain	200

No taper relief.

Next the shares are matched with the post 6.4.98 acquisition.

	£
Proceeds (2,000/5,000)	9,200
Less: cost (19.9.00)	(5,000)
Gain	4,200

No taper relief due.

Finally the shares are matched with the FA1985 pool.

	No	Cost	Indexed cost
		£	£
18.8.95	3,000	6,000	6,000
Index to April 1998			
£6,000 × 0.085			510
Pool at April 1998	3,000	6,000	6,510

	£
Disposal proceeds (2,000/5,000)	9,200
Less: cost (2,000/3,000 × £6,000)	(4,000)
	5,200
Less: indexation (2,000/3,000 (6,510 – 6,000))	(340)
Gain before taper relief	4,860
Gain after taper relief (85%)	£4,131

Yvonne's total gain before the annual exemption is £8,531.

(b)

	£
Capital gain on non-business asset	10,000
Less: capital loss in year	(6,000)
capital loss b/f	(4,000)
	–

	£
Capital gain on business asset	40,000
Less: capital loss b/f (£12,000 – £4,000)	(8,000)
Gain before taper relief	32,000
Gain after taper relief (25%)	£8,000

The losses are initially allocated to the gain on which no taper relief is due as this maximises the taper relief on the other gain.

The gain remaining chargeable after taper relief and the annual exemption is £300 (£8,000 – £7,700).

(c)

Business use		
1.8.00 – 1.8.01	=	12 months
Non business use		
1.8.01 – 1.2.03	=	18 months
		30 months

Number of complete years of ownership 1.8.00 – 31.7.02 = 2 years

	£
Business element	
£50,000 × 12/30 × 25%	5,000
Non business element	
£50,000 × 18/30 × 100%	30,000
Gain after taper relief	35,000

Marking Guide		**Marks**	
(a)	Shares sold in next 30 days	1	
	Gain	1	
	Post April 1998 shares	1	
	Gain	1	
	FA 1985 pool shares	1	
	Gain	2	
	Total gain	1	
			8
(b)	Set losses against gain on non-business asset	1	
	Set balance of brought forward loss against gain on business asset	1	
	Taper relief after set off losses	1	
	Gain chargeable	1	
			4
(c)	Business/non business use	1	
	Ownership period of taper relief	1	
	Taper relief	1	
			3
			15

41 SUSAN WHITE

Pass marks. Losses are allocated to gains before taper relief is applied. They should be allocated to the gain which attracts the lowest amount of taper relief (ie where the highest percentage of the gain remains chargeable).

(a) The following shareholdings in trading companies qualify for CGT business asset taper relief.

(i) shares in unlisted companies;

(ii) shares in a company of which the shareholder is an officer or employee;

(iii) shares in a company in which the shareholder can exercise at least 5% of voting rights.

In addition, an employee of a non trading company qualifies for business asset taper relief on a disposal of his shareholding providing he (together with any connected persons) does not own more than 10 per cent of (generally) the voting rights in the company.

(b) *Capital gains 2002/03*

Red Ltd

£

5,000 shares (acquired within next 30 days)

Proceeds $\frac{5,000}{20,000} \times £55,000$ — 13,750

Less: cost — (15,000)

Loss — (1,250)

£

15,000 shares (post 6.4.98 acquisition)

Proceeds $\frac{15,000}{20,000} \times £55,000$ — 41,250

Less: cost $\frac{15,000}{25,000} \times 37,500$ — (22,500)

Gain before taper relief — 18,750

Taper relief period (2.6.01 – 1.7.02) = 1 year. 50% of any net gain will remain chargeable after taper relief.

Blue Ltd

£

MV (sale between connected persons) — 200,000

Less: cost — (18,000)

Unindexed gain — 182,000

Less: indexation allowance to April 1998 — (12,800)

Indexed gain — 169,200

Gain not available for gift relief £(70,000 – 18,000) — £52,000

Taper relief period (6.4.98 – 5.4.02) = 4 years

Gift relief £(169,200 – 52,000) — £117,200

Summary

	1 year taper £	4 year taper £
Gains	18,750	52,000
Less: loss (best use)	(1,250)	-
Net gains before taper relief	17,500	52,000
Gains after taper relief		
50% × £17,500	8,750	
25% × £52,000		13,000
Total gains £(8,750 + 13,000)		£21,750

42   MR EDWARDS

> **Pass marks**. You were required to prepare notes for a meeting, so you could put your answer in note format.

(a) **Registration for VAT**

- **A person making taxable supplies becomes liable to register for VAT if, in any period of up to 12 consecutive calendar months, the value of his taxable supplies (excluding VAT) exceeds £55,000. The person is required to notify HM Customs & Excise within 30 days of the end of the 12 month period. HM Customs & Excise will then register the person with effect from the end of the month following the 12 month period, or from an earlier date if they and the trader agree.**

- Turnover exceeded the registration limit of £55,000 by 31 October 2002 and registration was therefore necessary by 1 December 2002.

- Immediate registration is now necessary.

- There is a VAT liability on any sales made since 1 December 2002.

- VAT should be charged immediately and customers advised that VAT invoices will be issued when the VAT registration number is known.

- VAT on sales from 1 December to today (10 December) will have to be accounted for out of Mr Edward's profit margin.

(b) **Annual accounting**

- **The annual accounting scheme is available to traders whose taxable turnover (exclusive of VAT) for the twelve months starting on their application to join the scheme is not expected to exceed £600,000.**

- **Traders cannot usually apply to join the scheme until they have been registered for at least twelve months. However, if Mr Edwards has a taxable turnover of up to £100,000 he can join the scheme as soon as he is registered.**

- **At the end of the year the trader compiles an annual VAT return which must be submitted to HM Customs & Excise along with any balancing payment of VAT (see below) due by two months after the end of the year.**

- Throughout the year payments on account of VAT must be made by direct debit. The trader must pay 90% of the previous year's net VAT liability during the year by means of nine monthly payments commencing at the end of the fourth month of the year.

Marking guide		
		Marks
(a)		
	Turnover limit passed in October	3
	Immediate registration is due (effective date 1 December)	2
	Liability to VAT from 1 December	1
	VAT to be charged immediately and invoices later	2
	Sales 1.12 – 10.12	1
(b)	Annual accounting turnover limit	1
	12 month rule/£100,000 limit	2
	One return and due date	2
	Monthly payments on account	1
		15

43 PREPARATION QUESTION: BENEFITS

> **Pass marks**. It was important to note that the cars were acquired part way through the year and to time apportion the benefits accordingly.

(a) **The use of a private house which cost £120,000**

Two calculations are required.

(i) The living accommodation benefit

	£
Annual value	2,000
Less contribution by director	(2,000)
	0

(ii) The additional charge for expensive accommodation

£(120,000 − 75,000) × 5%   £2,250

The total benefit is £2,250.

(b) **The purchase of a company asset at an undervalue**

The **benefit is the greater** of:

(i) The **asset's current market value**, and

(ii) The **asset's market value when first provided, less the total benefits taxed during the period of use**.

The acquisition price paid by the director is deducted from whichever of (i) and (ii) is used.

	£	£
Market value when first provided		3,500
Less: taxed in 1998/99 (20% of market value)	700	
taxed in 1999/00 (20% of market value)	700	
taxed in 2000/01 (20%)	700	
taxed in 2001/02 (20%)	700	
		(2,800)
		700

The figure of £700 is taken (as greater than the current market value of £600).

Benefit taxed in 2002/03

	£
Initial market value minus benefits already taxed	700
Less amount paid by director	(600)
Benefit	100

(c) **A low-interest loan to a director to purchase a season ticket**

This non qualifying loan is exempt as the total of all non qualifying loans to this director does not exceed £5,000.

(d) **The provision of medical insurance**

The general measure of a benefit for an employee earning £8,500 or more a year or a director is the cost to the employer of providing it. The benefit is thus £800.

(e) **Mercedes car**

The car was available for only seven months of the year so the benefit must be on a time basis.

The taxable percentage is 15% for cars with a baseline CO_2 emissions figure of 165g/km. This % is increased by 1% for every additional 5g/km of CO_2 emissions. In this case the % is 35%.

£24,000 × 35% × 7/12   £4,900

(f) **Computer**

	£
£3,900 × 20%	780
Less: de minimis	(500)
	280

44 RITA

> **Pass marks.** Always take care to apportion car and fuel benefits correctly. The CO_2 emissions figure for the car is rounded down to the nearest five below. 165g/km is the baseline figure at which the taxable percentage is 15%. The percentage is increased by 1% for each 5g/km by which the CO_2 emissions figure exceeds 165g/km.

	£
Salary	48,000
Accommodation (W1)	21,200
Relocation (£12,000 – £8,000)	4,000
Loan (£10,000 × 5%)	500
Car (£18,500 × 15% × 8/12)	1,850
Fuel benefit (£2,850 × 8/12)	1,900
Schedule E	77,450

Workings

1 *Accommodation*

	£
Annual value (higher than rent paid)	4,000
Electricity	700
Gas	1,200
Water	500
Council tax	1,300
Repairs	3,500
Furniture (20% × £30,000 × 6/12)	3,000
Purchase (W2)	7,000
	21,200

2 *Purchase of furniture*

Benefit is the higher of:

	£
(i) Cost	30,000
Less: taxed	(3,000)
	27,000
Less: amount paid	(20,000)
	7,000
(ii) Market value	25,000
Less: amount paid	(20,000)
	5,000

ie £7,000

Marking Guide	Marks
Salary	1
Annual value of property	1
Ancillary services	2
Relocation expenses	1
Use of furniture	1
Furniture (W2)	2
Loan benefit	2
Car benefit	3
Fuel benefit	2
	15

45   JOSEPHINE

> **Pass marks**. The calculation of car and fuel benefits are very important as they are often examined.

(a)   Class 1 primary contributions payable by Josephine

$10\% \times £(402 - 89) \times 52$ £1,627.60

Class 1 secondary contributions - payable by employer

$11.8\% \times £(402 - 89) \times 52$ £1,920.57

Class 1A contributions - payable by employer

$£6,850$ (W1) $\times 11.8\%$ £808.30

Note. **Childcare is exempt from Class 1 NICs provided it arises as a result of a contract made by the employer, not just reimbursed to the employee.**

Working

1   **Benefits**

		£
Car 1	$£12,000 \times 8/12 \times 25\%$	2,000
Car 2	$£21,000 \times 4/12 \times 15\%$	1,050
Fuel - Car 1	$£2,850 \times 8/12$	1,900
Fuel - Car 2	$£4,200 \times 4/12$	1,400
Medical insurance		500
		6,850

Note. For Car 1, the CO_2 emissions figure is rounded down to 200g/km. The baseline percentage is increased by 1% for each multiple of 5g/km above 165g/km. In this case $15\% + 7\% = 22\%$.

The percentage is then increased by 3% because the car is a diesel-engined car.

```
Marking guide
                                                      Marks
Class 1A - benefits in kind                              1
Class 1 - employer                                       1
Class 1 - employee                                       1
Childcare                                                2
                                                         5
Working
    Car 1
    25%                                                  3
    Time apportion                                       1
                                                         4

    Car 2
    15%                                                  2
    Time apportion                                       1
                                                         3

    Fuel - Car 1                                         1
    Fuel - Car 2                                         1
    Medical insurance                                    1
                                                         3
                                                        15
```

46 MR K

Pass marks. It was important to spot that each of the motor cars was only available for part of the tax year and to time apportion the benefit accordingly.

(a) (i) **Mercedes car**

		£
Car benefit £24,000 × 4/12 × 15%	1,200	
Fuel benefit £4,200 × 4/12	1,400	
		2,600

Lexus car

Car benefit £36,000 × 6/12 × 25%	4,500	
Fuel benefit £4,200 × 6/12	2,100	
		6,600

Legal costs and fine

Amount paid by company	1,200	
Less: contribution	(300)	
		900

(ii) **Suits**

2 × £800 × 20%	320

(iii) **Housing**

Annual rate	8,000	
Less: rent	(5,000)	
		3,000
Additional benefit		
(£125,000 - £75,000) × 5%		2,500
Total benefits in kind		15,920

(b) **The company must pay Class 1A NICS at 11.8% in respect of all of the benefits provided to Mr K:**

$11.8\% \times £15,920 = £1,878.56$

(c) MEMO

To: Board of Q Ltd
From: Certified accountant
Date: 31 March 2003
Subject: Annual cash bonuses to directors

The payment of cash bonuses to the directors will result in a Class 1 NIC charge for the company.

The director will be liable to income tax under PAYE on the bonus paid plus if the director's other cash remuneration is below the Class 1 NIC earnings upper limit then he/she will be liable for Class 1 NIC until that limit is reached.

Q Ltd will be responsible for collecting the director's PAYE and NIC due as well as accounting for its own NIC liability to the Inland Revenue.

Any amounts of tax and national insurance contributions that Q Ltd is liable to deduct during each tax month ending on the 5th are due for payment to the Collector of Taxes not later than 14 days after the month ends, ie by the 19th of each month.

Schedule E is taxed on the receipts basis. Thus the PAYE due will be collected on the date the bonus is deemed to be received by the director.

The time emoluments are received is the earliest of:

(i)   The date of the actual payment of, or on account of, emoluments, or

(ii) The date an individual becomes entitled to such a payment.

However, in the case of directors, they are deemed to have received emoluments on the earliest of potentially five dates which are the two dates already outlined plus the following three dates.

(iii) The date when sums on account of emoluments are credited in the accounts

(iv) The end of a period of account, where emoluments are determined before the end of the period, and

(v)   The date when the amount of emoluments for a period are determined if that is after the end of that period.

Signed: Certified Accountant

47   ERICA

> **Pass marks.** Note that benefits in kind still do not result in national insurance contributions being payable by employees. Payments in excess of the statutory mileage rates, however, are treated as earnings rather than a benefit in kind and so are subject to Class 1 contributions.

Employer A

Summary

	£
Salary plus bonus	26,250
Mileage 3,000 × £0.50	1,500
	27,750
Less: income tax (W1)	(4,595)
national insurance (W2)	(2,194)
Net income	20,961

Workings

1

	Non-savings Income £
Salary	25,000
Bonus @ 5%	1,250
	26,250
Statutory mileage rates 3,000 × (50 – 40p) taxable benefit	300
STI	26,550
Less: PA	(4,615)
Taxable income	21,935

Tax

	£
£1,920 × 10%	192
£(21,935 – 1,920) = £20,015 × 22%	4,403
Income tax liability	4,595

2   Earnings for Class 1 NICs (includes mileage rates) are £26,550

Class 1 primary liability is £(26,550 – 4,615) = £21,935 × 10%   2,194

Employer B

Summary

	£
Salary	22,000
Less: income tax (W1)	(4,912)
national insurance (W2)	(1,739)
Net income	15,349

Workings

1

	Non-savings Income £
Salary	22,000
Car benefit £12,000 × 25%	3,000
Fuel benefit	2,240
Computer £2,000 × 20% = £400, less than £500	0
Interest free loan less than £5,000	0
Medical insurance	750
STI	27,990
Less: PA	(4,615)
Taxable income	23,375

Note. To calculate the car benefit, round the CO_2 emissions figure down to 215g/km. Then increase the baseline percentage of 15% by 1% for each 5g/km of CO_2 emissions above the baseline figure of 165g/km.

BPP
PROFESSIONAL EDUCATION

Tax

		£
£1,920 × 10%		192
£(23,375 – 1,920) = £21,455 × 22%		4,720
Income tax liability		4,912

2   Earnings for Class 1 NICs are £22,000 (no Class 1A contributions for employees)

Class 1 primary liability is £(22,000 – 4,615) = 17,385 × 10%   1,739

Marking guide			
			Marks
(a)	Salary and bonus	1	
	Statutory mileage rates	2	
	Income tax computation	2	
	National insurance computation	1	
		—	
			6
(b)	Salary	1	
	Car benefit	1	
	Fuel benefit	1	
	Computer	1	
	Loan	1	
	Medical insurance	1	
	Income tax computation	2	
	National insurance computation	1	
		—	
			9
			15

48   SASHA SHAH

Pass marks.

1   Strictly, expenses are only deductible for Schedule E if they are incurred wholly, necessarily and exclusively in the performance of the duties. In practice, however, the Revenue allow an apportionment between private and business use as here.

2   Capital allowances are available to an employee who provides plant and machinery necessarily for use in the performance of his duties, in the same way as a sole trader.

3   The use of the car for travel between home and work is ordinary commuting and not business use.

(a)   Factors that will indicate that a worker should be treated as an employee rather than as self employed are:

(i)   control by employer over employee's work;

(ii)   employee must accept further work if offered (and employer must offer work);

(iii)   employee does not provide own equipment;

(iv)   employee does not hire own helpers;

(v)   employee does not take substantial financial risk;

(vi)   employee does not have responsibility for investment and management of business and cannot benefit from sound management;

(vii)   employee cannot work when he chooses but when an employer tells him to work;

(viii)   described as an employee in any agreement between parties.

(b) (i) Class 2 and Class 4 NIC 2002/03

		£
Class 2	£2 × 52	104
Class 4	£(30,420 – 4,615) × 7%	1,806
	Total	1,910

(ii) Class 1 NIC (Primary) 2002/03

£(30,420 – 4,615) × 10% = £2,581

(c) (i) Income assessable under Schedule D Case II 2002/03.

		£	£
Gross income			60,000
Less:	business expenses on heating etc	600	
	FYA @ 100% on computer	8,000	
	business expenses re car (£3,500 × 40%)	1,400	
	WDA @ 25% on business car		
	£10,000 × 25% × 40%	1,000	(11,000)
Assessable under Schedule D Case II			49,000

(ii) Income assessable under Schedule E 2002/03

	£	£
Gross income		60,000
Less: business expenses on heating etc (note 1)	600	
FYA @ 100% on computer (note 2)	8,000	(8,600)
Assessable under Schedule E		51,400

49 MR ROYLE

> **Pass marks.** The mention of losses in the question should lead you to consider whether it is possible to utilise them in future.

1 High Street
Anywhere

Mr J Royle
Blues House
Anywhere

[Date]

Dear Mr Royle

Purchase of business

Thank you for your enquiry about your proposed purchase. I will outline the advantages of either buying the assets of the business or shares in the company.

Purchase of assets

(a) You will be able to choose which assets you wish to acquire, rather than the whole of the assets of the company.

(b) You will be entitled to claim **capital allowances on plant and machinery, including a possible first year allowance of 40%. Industrial buildings allowance may also be available on the factory**.

(c) It may be possible to **maximise the use of capital allowances by allocating consideration to assets which attract more capital allowances,** eg plant and machinery.

(d) The liabilities of the company will not be passed to you.

(e) One disadvantage is that you **will not be able to utilise the existing losses of the company**.

(f) **VAT may be chargeable on the assets** acquired by you. If you cannot fully recover all the VAT paid on acquiring the assets, this may be unattractive.

There is a relief which provides that VAT is not chargeable on the transfer of a business as a going concern, but this may not be available if you only purchase some of the assets.

Purchase of shares

(a) The business of the company will continue uninterrupted.

(b) You will be taking over the liabilities of the company as well as the assets.

(c) **Capital allowances and industrial buildings allowance will be unaffected** by the purchase. However, this means that there will be no first year allowance available.

(d) It may be possible **for the losses incurred by the company to be carried forward** and used against profits in future years.

However, **where there is a change ownership of a company and a major change in the nature of the conduct of the company's trade occurs within three years, trading losses cannot be carried forward**. This also applies where there is a change in ownership after the scale of activities has become small or negligible before it revives.

I suggest we meet to discuss your proposed purchase further.

Yours sincerely,

Certified Accountant

Marking guide		Marks
Layout		1
(a)	Choice of assets	1
	Capital allowances	2
	Consideration	1
	No liabilities	1
	No losses	1
	VAT charge	1
	TOGC relief	1
		8
(b)	Business carries on	1
	Liabilities	1
	Capital allowances	1
	Losses used	1
	Restriction on losses	2
		6
		15

50 MRS DOUGLAS

> **Pass marks**. A combination of remuneration and dividends is usually best.

(a) (i) **Bonus**

Income tax 2002/03

	Non savings income £	Total £
Salary	4,800	
Bonus	10,000	
STI	14,800	14,800
Less: PA	(4,615)	
Taxable income	10,185	10,185

Tax

	£
£1,920 × 10%	192
£8,265 (10,185 – 1,920) × 22%	1,818
	2,010

National insurance – Class 1
£ (14,800 – 4,615) × 10% =   £1,019

Net income after tax and NICs
£(14,800 – 2,010 – 1,019) =   £11,771

(ii)

	Non savings income £	Dividend income £	Total £
Salary	4,800		
Dividend £10,000 × 100/90		11,111	
STI	4,800	11,111	15,911
Less: PA	(4,615)		
Taxable income	185	11,111	11,296

Tax

	£
£185 × 10%	19
£11,111 × 10%	1,111
	1,130
Less: tax credit on dividend	(1,111)
Tax liability	19

National insurance – Class 1
£185 (4,800 – 4,615) × 10% =   19

Net income after tax and NICs
£(4,800 + 10,000 – 19 – 19) =   14,762

(b) **A combination of dividends and remuneration usually gives the best result.**

Remuneration and the cost of benefits are allowed as deductions in computing the company's profits chargeable to corporation tax. This could affect the rate of corporation tax.

A certain minimum amount of salary should be paid out to protect National Insurance benefits and also to use the income tax personal allowance.

Marking guide

			Marks	
(a)	(i)	Salary and bonus	1	
		Taxable income	1	
		Tax liability	1	
		NICs	1	
		Net income after tax	1	
				5
	(ii)	Salary and dividend	2	
		Taxable income	1	
		Tax liability	1	
		Tax credit	1	
		NICs	1	
		Net income after tax	1	
				7
(b)		Combination of salary/divis	1	
		Reduction for company	1	
		NI benefits/use of personal allowance	1	
				3
				15

Business Taxation
Mock Exam 1

Question Paper:	
Time allowed	**3 hours**

paper 2.3

DO NOT OPEN THIS PAPER UNTIL YOU ARE READY TO START
UNDER EXAMINATION CONDITIONS

SECTION A – BOTH questions are compulsory and MUST be attempted

51   UNFORSEEN UPSETS LIMITED

Unforeseen Upsets Limited (UUL) is a United Kingdom resident company which has been manufacturing lifeboats for many years. It has no associated companies. The company has previously made up accounts to 31 December but has now changed its accounting date to 31 March.

The company's results for the 15 month period to 31 March 2003 are as follows.

	£
Trading profits (as adjusted for taxation but before capital allowances)	1,125,000
Bank interest receivable (note 4)	20,000
Debenture interest receivable (note 5)	17,500
Chargeable gain (notes 6 and 7)	30,000
Gift aid donation paid (note 8)	20,000
Dividends received from UK companies (note 9)	6,300

Notes

1   UUL is a small company with a turnover in the period of account ended 31 March 2003 of £2,000,000. The company has 30 employees.

2   *Capital allowances - plant and machinery*

On 1 January 2002 the tax written-down values of plant and machinery were:

	£
Pool	142,000

Sales during the accounting period were:

		£
31.7.02	3 cars	15,000
30.9.02	Plant and machinery	12,000

Additions during the accounting period were:

		£
1.6.02	1 car	14,000
1.8.02	3 cars (£8,000 each)	24,000
30.11.02	Plant and machinery	92,000
28.2.03	Computer equipment	2,400

3   On 1 January 2002 the company had trading losses brought forward of £600,000.

4   *Bank interest receivable*

	£
31.3.02 received	3,000
30.6.02 received	4,000
30.9.02 received	5,000
31.12.02 received	8,000
	20,000

All interest was received at the end of the quarter for which accrued. The bank interest was non trading income.

5   *Debenture interest receivable (gross amounts)*

	£
30.9.02 received	10,500
31.3.03 received	7,000
	17,500

(a)   The loan was made on 1 July 2002.

(b)   £1,500 was accrued at 31 December 2002. There was no accrual at 31 March 2003. ~~make adjustment~~

(c)   The interest was non-trading income.

(d)   The interest was received gross from another UK company.

6   The chargeable gain was realised on 1 July 2002.

7   On 1 January 2002 the company had capital losses brought forward of £50,000.

8   *Gift aid donations paid*   *chargeable gain.*

	£
31.5.02	7,000
31.10.02	4,000
28.2.03	9,000
	20,000

9   *Dividends received*

28.2.03	£6,300

Required

(a)   **Calculate the mainstream corporation tax payable for the fifteen month period of account.**   (20 marks)

(b)   **State the date(s) by which the company must pay its mainstream corporation tax liability, the date by which it must file return(s) and the penalties due if returns are not filed by the due date.**   *p8*   (9 marks)

(c)   **State what unrelieved amounts are carried forward at 31 March 2003.**   (1 mark)

(30 marks)

52   **MARIO AND MARISA**

Mario and Marisa married in 1988. Mario is now 45 and Marisa is 42.

In 2002/03 Mario received a salary from his employer of £27,749. Mario was provided with a company car by his employer. Until 5 September 2002 he had the use of a 1800cc petrol car whose list price was £10,500 which had a CO_2 emissions figure of 166g/km. On 6 September 2002 the car was changed for a 2300 cc new diesel car with a list price of £16,000. The diesel car had a CO_2 emissions figure of 204g/km.

All fuel was paid for by his employer.

On 6 October 2001 Mario was provided with a computer for both business and private use at home. The computer cost Mario's employer £3,000 on 6 October 2001.

Mario received bank interest from Lloyds Bank of £120 on 30 June 2002.

Mario and Marisa moved into a new home on 6 April 2002. The purchase of the house was funded by a loan of £20,000 from Mario's employer on which annual interest of 2% was payable.

Marisa has made a capital gain in 2002/03. The gain arose on the disposal of a business asset that had been owned since August 1995. The cost of the asset was £13,825 and the proceeds were £73,000. The indexation factor to April 1998 was 0.085.

Marisa has carried on a garment manufacturing business since June 1998. She makes up annual accounts to 31 March. The adjusted trading profit before capital allowances to 31 March 2003 was £49,500 and the capital allowances on plant and machinery were £2,500. On 1 April 2000 she purchased a new factory for £100,000 which was immediately brought into use. On 30 September 2002 Marisa sold the factory for £55,000. The factory was always used in the business.

Required

Calculate the tax liabilities for the year 2002/03 of:

(a) Mario; and   (13 marks)

(b) Marisa   (12 marks)

Assume that the official rate of interest is 5%.   **(25 marks)**

SECTION B - THREE questions ONLY to be attempted

53   FLAT RATE SCHEME AND ANNUAL ACCOUNTING

Cliché Ltd is a company which provides high class laundry services. All sales are standard rated and are made to individual customers.

For the year to 31 March 2003 Cliché Ltd made sales of £220,000 (incl VAT).

Cliché Ltd's standard rated expenses in the year to 31 March 2003 amounted to £15,100.

Required

(a)   Calculate how much VAT Cliché Ltd will have to pay for the year using:

    (i)   the normal basis of calculating VAT   (2 marks)

    (ii)   the flat rate scheme and assuming the relevant flat rate percentage is 12%.   (1 mark)

(b)   State what the advantages of using the flat rate scheme are.   (4 marks)

(c)   State the conditions that a company must meet before it can use the annual accounting scheme and what the consequences of using the schemes are.

                        (8 marks)

                        (15 marks)

54   P LTD

(a)   On 5 July 2002, P Ltd sold 17,500 ordinary shares in T Ltd for £140,000. These shares were part of holding of 22,500 (a 5% holding) shares which had been acquired as follows:

Date	Shares	Cost £
Pool at 5.4.85	15,000	60,000 (indexed cost £64,000)
April 1996	1 for 3 rights issue	£4 per share
29 June 2002	2,500	18,750

Required

Compute the chargeable gain arising as a result of this disposal   (9 marks)

(b)   The managing director of G Ltd has decided that his company should acquire 80% of the share capital of H Ltd, a company in the same trade. On examining the latest balance sheet of H Ltd, he noted that its premises were valued at £60,000. He considers that this property will be surplus to the company's requirements and that it could be sold for £150,000 once his company has acquired H Ltd thus providing valuable working capital. On making further enquiries he establishes that the property had cost H Ltd £40,000 in March 1991 and that H Ltd had rolled over a previous gain of £10,000 against the cost.

Required

On the assumption that H Ltd is acquired in April 2002 and that the property is sold in July 2002, advise the managing director of the amount of additional funds that will be generated, after paying any corporation tax on the resulting gain. H Ltd's other taxable profits will be approximately £350,000 for the year ended 31 March 2003.   (6 marks)

                        (15 marks)

55 J LTD

J Ltd is a UK-resident company which has three wholly-owned UK subsidiary companies. In addition, it holds 5% of the shares of P Inc and 6% of the shares of L Inc. Both these companies are non-UK resident companies.

The following information concerning J Ltd relates to the 12-month accounting period ended on 31 March 2003.

	£	£
UK trading profits		600,000
Schedule D Case V: overseas dividends from P Inc (after withholding tax at 25%)	37,500	
overseas dividends from L Inc (after withholding tax at 10%)	36,000	
		73,500
Gift aid donation		12,000

Required

(a) Compute the MCT payable by J Ltd for the above period showing clearly your treatment of foreign tax. (11 Marks)

(b) Explain briefly how the computation would have differed had the holdings in the foreign companies been 10%. You are not required to re-calculate the figures. (4 Marks)

(15 marks)

56 SOLE TRADER V COMPANIES

You are required, briefly, to contrast the income tax, national insurance and pension funding consequences of a taxpayer commencing a trade in January 2003 as:

(a) a sole trader; and
(b) a director of his own company. **(15 marks)**

57 LOSSES AND CHANGE OF ACCOUNTING DATE

(a) A trader (a single person) has a trading loss for the year to 31 December 2002 of £18,000. He made a trading profit of £2,500 for the year to 31 December 2001. Other income, gains and losses were as follows:

	2001/02 £	2002/03 £
Other income	2,500	2,900
Capital gains	–	26,000
Capital losses	–	2,000

Capital losses brought forward at 6 April 2000 are £4,700.
Taper relief is not due in respect of the capital gain.

His adjusted trading profits for the year to 31 December 2003 show a breakeven position.

Required

Show how the loss for the year to 31 December 2002 should be relieved, explaining your reasons and showing any trading and/or capital loss carried forward. **(9 marks)**

Use the rates and allowances for 2002/03 for both years.

115

(b)   Sue is a self-employed secretary. She commenced trading on 1 September 1999 and initially made up accounts to 31 December each year. However, in 2003 she changed her accounting date to 31 March.

Sue's results have been:

	£
1.9.99 – 31.12.99	16,000
1.1.00 – 31.12.00	48,000
1.1.01 – 31.12.01	36,000
1.1.02 – 31.12.02	42,000
1.1.03 – 31.3.03	15,000

Required

Calculate the amounts chargeable to income tax for 1999/00 to 2002/03.

(6 marks)

(15 marks)

MOCK EXAM 1: ANSWERS

DO NOT TURN THIS PAGE UNTIL YOU HAVE COMPLETED THE MOCK EXAM

WARNING! APPLYING OUR MARKING SCHEME

If you decide to mark your paper using our marking scheme, you should bear in mind the following points.

1   The BPP solutions are not definitive: you will see that we have applied the marking scheme to our solutions to show how good answers should gain marks, but there may be more than one way to answer the question. You must try to judge fairly whether different points made in your answers are correct and relevant and therefore worth marks according to our marking scheme.

2   If you have a friend or colleague who is studying or has studied this paper, you might ask him or her to mark your paper for you, thus gaining a more objective assessment. Remember you and your friend are not trained or objective markers, so try to avoid complacency or pessimism if you appear to have done very well or very badly.

3   You should be aware that BPP's answers are longer than you would be expected to write. Sometimes, therefore, you would gain the same number of marks for making the basic point as we have shown as being available for a slightly more detailed or extensive solution.

It is most important that you analyse your solutions in detail and that you attempt to be as objective as possible.

A PLAN OF ATTACK

What's the worst thing you could be doing right now if this was the actual exam paper? Sharpening your pencil? Wondering how to celebrate the end of the exam in 2 hours 59 minutes time? Panicking, flapping and generally getting in a right old state?

Well, they're all pretty bad, so turn back to the paper and let's sort out a **plan of attack**!

First things first

Spend a good 5 minutes looking through the paper in detail working out which optional questions to do and the order in which to attack the questions. You've then got **two options**.

Option 1 (if you're thinking 'Help!')

If you're a bit worried about the paper, do the questions in the order of how well you think you can answer them. You will probably find the optional questions in Section B less daunting than the compulsory questions in Section A so start with Section B.

- The requirements of **question 53** are broken down, which is helpful in allocating your time. Also, you can clearly see where the marks are. If you like VAT and could answer each part of the question this may well have been worth doing. Answer the question in 27 minutes.

- If you are totally happy with chargeable gains calculations then start with **question 54**. If you feel you are doing these computations correctly, it will boost your confidence. However, before you choose a question with two parts like this, ensure you can answer both parts.

- **Question 55** is another mainly computational question. If you are happy with overseas matters and you like the computations this question could give you another confidence boost. Allow yourself 27 minutes to answer the question and make sure that you leave 7 minutes to answer the written part (b).

- **Question 56** is a written question. This is a fairly standard question and, if you like written questions, you might have well been advised to do this. Ensure you answer all three aspects of the question.

- **Question 57** is a fairly straightforward losses and change of accounting date question. If you feel confident with these computations you should have selected this question. However, you should not have selected the question unless you could answer both parts of it.

When you've spent the allocated time on the three questions in Section B turn to the compulsory questions in Section A. You should have 1 hour and 30 minutes left at this point in the exam. Read the compulsory questions through thoroughly before you launch into them. Once you start make sure you allocate your time to the parts within the questions according to the marks available and that, where possible, you attempt the easy marks first.

Lastly, what you mustn't forget is that you have to **answer both questions in Section A, and THREE questions from Section B**. Once you've decided on your three questions from Section B, it might be worth putting a line through the other questions so that you are not tempted to answer them!

Option 2 (if you're thinking 'It's a doddle')

It never pays to be over confident but if you're not quaking in your shoes about the exam then **turn straight to the compulsory questions** in Section A. You've got to do them so you might as well get them over and done with.

Once you've done the compulsory questions, choose three of the questions in Section B.

- If you prefer working with numbers rather than providing written answers it might be best to avoid **question 56** in Section B.

- Your choice from the other questions really depends on what you are most confident at. The other questions are all fairly standard computational questions.

No matter how many times we remind you....

Always, always **allocate your time** according to the marks for the question in total and then according to the parts of the question. And **always, always follow the requirements** exactly. Question 57, for example, asks you to explain your reasons for claiming loss relief. So give an explanation.

You've got spare time at the end of the exam.....?

If you have allocated your time properly then you **shouldn't have time on your hands** at the end of the exam. But if you find yourself with five or ten minutes to spare, check over your work to make sure that there are no silly arithmetical errors.

Forget about it!

And don't worry if you found the paper difficult. More than likely other candidates will too. If this were the real thing you would need to **forget** the exam the minute you leave the exam hall and **think about the next one**. Or, if it's the last one, **celebrate**!

51   **UNFORSEEN UPSETS LIMITED**

> **Pass marks**. Break a long question like this down into manageable parts in order to gain the easy marks. It is essential that you are aware that a long period of account is split into two accounting periods and that the first period is always twelve months in length. If you do not make this split correctly you cannot hope to pass the question.

(a) **Corporation tax computations**

	Year to 31.12.02 £	3 months to 31.3.03 £
Trading profits	900,000	225,000
Less: capital allowances (W1)	(74,550)	(13,054)
	825,450	211,946
Less: losses b/f	(600,000)	
	225,450	211,946
Schedule D Case III (W2)	32,000	5,500
Chargeable gains (W3)	–	–
	257,450	217,446
Less: charges paid	(11,000)	(9,000)
PCTCT	246,450	208,446
Dividends plus tax credits £6,300 × 100/90	–	7,000
'Profits' for small companies rate purposes	246,450	215,446

Corporation tax (W4)

	£	£
FY 01		
£246,450 × 3/12 × 20%	12,323	
FY 02		
£246,450 × 9/12 × 19%	35,119	
FY 02		
£208,446 × 30%		62,534
Less: Small companies marginal relief		
11/400 (£375,000 – £215,446) × $\dfrac{208,446}{215,446}$		(4,245)
	47,442	58,289

(b) £47,442 in respect of the 12 months to 31.12.02 must be paid by 1 October 2003.

£58,289 in respect of the 3 months to 31.3.03 must be paid by 1 January 2004.

A return for the 12 months to 31.12.02 and a return for the 3 months to 31.3.03 must be filed by 31.3.04.

If a return is filed late there is an initial penalty of £100. This rises to £200 if the return is more than 3 months late. These penalties rise to £500 and £1,000 respectively for the third consecutive late filing of a return.

There is in addition a tax geared penalty, if the return is more than six months late. The penalty is 10% of the tax unpaid six months after the return was due if the total delay is up to 12 months, but it increases to 20% of that tax if the return is over 12 months late.

(c) At 31 March 2003 there are capital losses to carry forward of £20,000 (W3).

Workings

1 **Capital allowances**

	FYA £	Pool £	Expensive Car £	Allowances £
Year to 31.12.02				
TWDV b/f		142,000		
Additions		24,000	14,000	
Disposals		(27,000)		
		139,000	14,000	
WDA @ 25%/(restricted)		(34,750)	(3,000)	37,750
Additions	92,000			
FYA @ 40%	(36,800)			36,800
		55,200		74,550
TWDV c/f		159,450	11,000	
3 months to 31.3.03				
WDA @ 25%/(restricted) × 3/12		(9,966)	(688)	10,654
Additions	2,400			
FYA @ 100%	(2,400)			2,400
				13,054
		0		
		149,484	10,312	

Note. As Unforeseen Upsets Ltd is **a small enterprise it is entitled to FYAs of 100% on the computer equipment and FYAs of 40% on the plant and machinery**.

2 **Schedule D Case III**

The interest is taxable under Schedule D Case III on an accruals basis:

	Year to 31.12.02 £	3 months to 31.3.03 £
Bank interest	20,000	–
Debenture interest	12,000	5,500
	32,000	5,500

3 **Chargeable gains**

	Year to 31.12.02 £
Gain	30,000
Loss/b/f	(30,000)
Net gain	-

The loss c/f on 1.4.03 is £20,000 (£50,000 – £30,000).

4 **Corporation tax**

Year to 31.12.02

The year to 31.12.02 straddles FY 01 and FY 02. The small companies rate lower limit for both years is £300,000 so the small companies' rate applies to both financial years.

3 months to 31.3.03

	FY 02 (3/12) £
Profits	215,446
PCTCT	208,446
Lower limit for small companies rate	75,000
Upper limit for small companies rate	375,000

Small companies marginal relief applies.

Marking guide		**Marks**
(a)	Division of trading profit	1
	Trading losses brought forward	1
	Bank interest	1
	Debenture interest	1
	Capital gains/losses	1
	Charges on income – Gift Aid Donation	1
	Working 1 - Capital allowances	
	CAP to 31.12.02	
	Sales and additions	1
	WDA	1
	FYA	1
	CAP to 31.3.03	
	WDA	1
	FYA	1
	CAP to 31.12.02	
	Calculation of 'P'	1
	Recognition of applicable small companies rate	1
	Tax calculation	2
	CAP to 31.3.03	
	Calculation of 'P'	1
	Calculation of reduced limits	1
	Recognition of applicable marginal relief	1
	Calculation of liability	2
		20
(b)	Due dates for payment	2
	For returns	2
	Penalties	5
		9
(c)	Capital losses	1
		30

52   MARIO AND MARISA

Pass marks. The first £500 of any benefit arising in respect of the private use of computer equipment is exempt.

(a)   **Mario - income tax liability**

	Non-savings £	Savings (excl dividend £	Total £
Schedule E (W1)	35,076	0	
Bank interest (£120 × 100/80)		150	
Statutory total income	35,076	150	35,226
Less: Personal allowance	(4,615)		
	30,461	150	30,611

Income tax on non-savings income

	£
£1,920 × 10%	192
£27,980 × 22%	6,156
£561 × 40%	224

Income tax on savings (excl dividend) income

	£
£150 × 40%	60
Income tax liability	6,632

(b) **Marisa - income tax liability**

	£
Schedule D Case I (£49,500 – £2,500 – 37,000 (W2))	10,000
Less: Personal allowance	(4,615)
Taxable income	5,385

	£
Income tax on non-savings income	
£1,920 × 10%	192
£3,465 × 22%	762
Income tax liability	954

Capital gains tax liability

	£
Gains after taper relief (25%) (W3)	14,500
Less: annual exemption	(7,700)
	6,800

£6,800 × 20% = £1,360.

Workings

1   **Schedule E**

	£
Salary	27,749
Car 1 (£10,500 × 15%) × 5/12	656
Car 2 (£16,000 × 25%) × 7/12	2,333
Fuel benefit	
Car 1 £2,850 × 5/12	1,188
Car 2 £4,200 × 7/12	2,450
Computer equipment (£3,000 × 20% - £500)	100
Beneficial loan (£20,000 × 5% – 2%)	600
	35,076

Note. The taxable percentage for the diesel car is calculated by rounding down the CO_2 emission figure to 200g/km. The % of 15% is then increased by 1% for each 5g/km that CO_2 emissions exceed 165g/km. 3% is added because the car is a diesel car.

2   **Industrial buildings allowance**

	£
Cost	100,000
WDA at 4%	
y/e 31.3.01	(4,000)
y/e 31.3.02	(4,000)
Residue before sale	92,000

Balancing allowance

	£
Residue before sale	92,000
Less: proceeds	(55,000)
Balancing allowance	37,000

3   **Capital gain**

	£
Proceeds	73,000
Less: cost	(13,825)
Unindexed gain	59,175
Less: indexation allowance	
0.085 × £13,825	(1,175)
Indexed gain	58,000
Gain after taper relief (25%)	£14,500

Marking guide

			Marks
(a)	(i)	Bank interest	1
		Income tax calculation	2
			3
(b)	(i)	Schedule D Case I	1
	(ii)	Taper relief	1
		Annual exemption	1
		Capital gains tax calculation	4
		Tax	1
			8

Working 1
Car 1	
Taxable percentage	$2\frac{1}{2}$
Age reduction	1
Time reduction	1
Car 2	
Taxable percentage	$1\frac{1}{2}$
Time reduction	1
Fuel benefit	
Car 1	1
Car 2	1
Computer equipment	1
Beneficial loan	1
	10

Working 2
Allowances claimed	2
Balancing allowance	2
	4
	25

53   **FLAT RATE SCHEME AND ANNUAL ACCOUNTING**

> **Pass marks**. The flat rate scheme was introduced by Finance Act 2002 and should therefore be considered to be a highly likely exam topic in 2003.

(a)   (i)   **Input VAT**

	£
Output VAT	
(£220,000 × 17.5/117.5)	32,766
Less: Input VAT	
(£15,100 × 17.5/117.5)	(2,249)
VAT payable	30,517

      (ii)   **Flat rate scheme**

          £220,000 × 12%   £26,400

(b)   The advantages of using the flat rate scheme to Cliché Ltd are:

      (i)   **VAT of £4,117** (£30,517 – £26,400) **is saved**.

      (ii)   **VAT administration is simplified.**

      (iii)   As none of Cliché Ltd's customers are VAT registered **there will be no need** to **issue VAT invoices**.

(c)   Under the annual accounting scheme only **one VAT return is submitted each year**. The scheme can only be used if the **expected taxable turnover** for the next 12 months **does not exceed £600,000**.

      Businesses with a turnover of less than £100,000 can join the annual accounting scheme as soon as they register for VAT. Businesses with a turnover of over £100,000 have to wait until they have been VAT registered for at least 12 months before they can use the scheme.

      Most businesses using the annual accounting scheme make nine monthly payments on account. Any balancing payment is made with the VAT return two months after the end of the year.

Marking guide

			Marks
(a)	(i)	Input VAT: normal calculation	2
	(ii)	Input VAT: flat rate scheme	1
			3
(b)		Advantages	4
(c)		Turnover does not exceed £600,000	2
		12 month wait/£100,000 limit	2
		Payments on account	2
		Annual tax return	2
			8
			15

---

54   P LTD

Pass marks. This was a straightforward computation of gains on the disposal of shares and assets subject to rollover relief.

(a)   P Ltd

                                               £

      Last nine days

      Proceeds

      $\dfrac{2,500}{17,500} \times £140,000$ 20,000

      Less: cost   (18,750)

      Gain   1,250

      No IA available

The FA 1985 pool

	No. £	Cost £	Indexed Cost
Pool at 5.4.85	15,000	60,000	64,000

April 1996
Indexation
$$\frac{152.6-94.8}{94.8} \times £64,000$$

			39,021
Acquisition rights 1 for 3	5,000	20,000	20,000
	20,000	80,000	123,021

July 2002
Indexation
$$\frac{174.8-152.6}{152.6} \times £123,021$$

			17,897
			140,918
Sale	(15,000)	(60,000)	(105,688)
c/f	5,000	20,000	35,230

Gain on 1985 pool

	£
Proceeds $\frac{15,000}{17,500} \times £140,000$	120,000
Less: cost	(60,000)
Unindexed gain	60,000
Less: indexation allowance £(105,688 – 60,000)	(45,688)
Indexed gain	14,312
Total gains £(1,250 + 14,312)	15,562

(b) **G Ltd**

The gain on the sale in July 2002 will be:

	£	£
Proceeds		150,000
Less: cost	40,000	
Less: rolled over gain	(10,000)	(30,000)
Unindexed gain		120,000
Less: indexation allowance		
$\frac{174.8-131.4}{131.4}$ (= 0.330) × £30,000		(9,900)
Indexed gain chargeable on H Ltd		110,100

As G Ltd and H Ltd are associated companies for the purposes of the small companies' rate of corporation tax, the limits are divided by two. The small companies lower limit is therefore £150,000 and the upper limit is £750,000. The capital gain will therefore be in the small companies marginal relief band and suffer 32.75% tax.

Tax @ 32.75%	36,058
Net proceeds of sale £(150,000 – 36,058)	113,942

Marking guide	
	Marks
Last 9 days disposal	2
FA 1985 pool	
- IA to 4.96	1
- rights issue	2
- IA to 7.02	1
- disposal	1
Calculation of gain	1
Total gains	<u>1</u>
	9
Proceeds less cost	1
Rolled over gain	1
IA	1
Small companies rate	1
Marginal relief	1
Net proceeds	<u>1</u>
	<u>6</u>
Total	<u>15</u>

55   J LTD

Pass marks. The three UK subsidiaries meant that small companies' marginal relief was unavailable, the upper limit being £1,500,000/4 = £375,000. This simplified the calculations considerably.

(a)

	Total £	UK profits £	P Inc £	L Inc £
Schedule D Case I	600,000	600,000		
Schedule D Case V				
£37,500 × 100/75	50,000		50,000	
£36,000 × 100/90	40,000			40,000
Less charges	(12,000)	(12,000)		
	678,000	588,000	50,000	40,000
Corporation tax at 30%	203,400	176,400	15,000	12,000
Less DTR: lower of				
UK tax (£15,000/12,000)				
Overseas (£12,500/£4,000)	(16,500)		(12,500)	(4,000)
Mainstream corporation tax	186,900	176,400	2,500	8,000

(b) **If the holdings had been 10%, underlying tax relief** (for the corporation tax suffered by the overseas companies) **would have been available,** in addition to relief for the withholding tax. Total relief would still be limited to the UK tax on the overseas profits. The overseas profits would have to be grossed up by the underlying tax as well as the withholding tax.

Underlying tax is calculated as:

$$\text{Gross dividend income} \times \frac{\text{Foreign tax paid}}{\text{After-tax accounting profits}}$$

Marking guide

		Marks
(a)	Sch DI	1
	Sch DV	2
	Charges – set off v UK income	2
	Corporation tax	2
	DTR - P Inc	2
	- L Inc	2
		11
(b)	Underlying tax relief	1
	Total relief	1
	Fraction	2
		4
		15

56   SOLE TRADER V COMPANIES

> **Pass marks.** It is important to plan answers to written questions such as this in order to ensure that you answer the question asked.

The factors set out below are of general importance in deciding whether to trade through a limited company or as a sole trader.

(a)   Tax on profits

The tax system makes no distinction between an individual and his business. Thus any profits a sole trader makes are aggregated with any other income he may have, irrespective of whether they are withdrawn from the business for personal use or retained in the business. Income tax on non-savings income is currently levied at a starting rate of 10% on the first £1,920, at a basic rate of 22% on the next £27,980 and, where taxable income exceeds £29,900, at a higher rate of 40% on the excess. So, if a business is likely to generate substantial profits, they will be taxed at a marginal rate of 40%. If the business starts in January 2003 profits arising from the commencement date until 5 April 2003 will be taxed in 2002/03.

A company's trading profits have no income tax implications for shareholders unless the company pays a dividend, when the gross dividend becomes part of the shareholder's total income for the tax year in which it was paid. Dividends received carry a tax credit of 10% which can be set against a taxpayer's tax liability. However, the tax credit cannot be repaid to non taxpayers. Dividends are treated as the top slice of income. They are taxed at 10% if they fall in the starting or basic rate bands and at 32.5% if they exceed the basic rate threshold of £29,900.

For a director receiving remuneration, the remuneration is subject to income tax under Schedule E in the hands of the director in the tax year that it is received.

(b)   Private expenditure and benefits paid for by the business

Private expenditure and benefits paid for by the business are disallowed in computing a sole trader's trading profits subject to income tax. Normally, however, such expenditure is deductible for corporation tax purposes. But, for directors of the company, any such expenditure will result in a charge to Schedule E income tax under the benefits in kind rules. Nevertheless some benefits, and in particular company cars, may still be attractive, since the full economic value of the asset is not reflected in the benefit charge.

(c) **The payment of tax liabilities**

Schedule D Case I income tax is payable on 31 January following the tax year, but with two payments on account (which normally cover most of the tax liability) on 31 January in the tax year and on the 31 July which is six months later. There is a 10% tax credit on dividends received by shareholders (although there will be no further liability for basic and starting rate taxpayers). Tax will be withheld from any remuneration under the Schedule E system.

For a small or medium sized company corporation tax is payable nine months after the end of the accounting period.

(d) **National insurance contributions**

A sole trader pays national insurance contributions under Class 2 and Class 4. Class 2 contributions are levied weekly at a flat rate (£2.00 a week for 2002/03). Class 4 contributions are payable at a rate of 7% on business profits (between £4,615 and £30,420 for 2002/03). The maximum Class 4 contribution payable is thus £1,806.

The remuneration of a director of a company is subject to Class 1 contributions. Employees pay contributions of 10% of earnings between the primary threshold of £4,615 and the upper earnings limit of £30,420. Employers pay contributions of 11.8% on earnings above the earnings threshold of £4,615. If the individual earns a substantial salary, the Class 1 contributions paid by the employer and employee combined are likely to be considerably greater than the contributions paid by a sole trader. However, the company's contributions are deductible in computing the company's trading profits. (The individual's gross salary, out of which he pays his contributions, is similarly deductible.)

There are no national insurance contributions on dividends.

(e) **Pension funding**

As a sole trader any pension would have to be provided by a personal pension plan funded by premiums paid by reference to age-determined percentages of net relevant earnings.

A company may however, decide to set up an Inland Revenue approved pension scheme under which contributions could be paid by both the company and the director. The company contributions would not be taxable benefits in kind for a director and a director's contributions would be allowed as a deduction in arriving at his taxable pay. Where there is no company pension scheme a director may take out a personal pension plan.

Marking Guide	Marks
Tax on business profits	2
Tax on company profits	2
Private expenditure	2
Income tax payment	2
CT due date	1
Class 2/4 NICs	2
Employee/Employer NICs	2
Pension funding	2
	15

57   LOSSES

> **Pass marks**. Remember to consider using the loss against gains as well as income.

2001/02

(a)   **It is clearly not beneficial to make a s 380 claim against total income as this would result in the loss of the personal allowance.**

Income

	£
Sch DI (y/e 31.12.01)	2,500
Other income	2,500
STI	5,000
Less: PA	(4,615)
Taxable income	385

2002/03

A s 380 claim should be made, even though this results in the loss of the personal allowance. This is because the loss can be set against the capital gain.

Income

	£
Other income	2,900
Less: loss relief	(2,900)
STI/taxable income	Nil

Gains

	£
Gain	26,000
Less: c/y loss	(2,000)
	24,000
Less: loss relief lower of	
(i) £(18,000 – 2,900) = £15,100;	
(ii) £(24,000 – 4,700) = £19,300	
ie	(15,100)
	8,900
Less: losses b/f	(1,200)
	7,700
Less: annual exemption	(7,700)
	Nil
Losses to c/f £(4,700 – 1,200)	£3,500

No trading loss to carry forward

(b)

1999/00
1.9.99 – 5.4.00
£16,000 + (3/12 × £48,000)   £28,000
2000/01   £48,000
y/e 31.12.00
2001/02   £36,000
y/e 31.12.01

Overlap profits are £12,000.

2002/03

1.1.02 – 31.3.03		
42,000 + 15,000 (15 months)		57,000
Less: overlap profits (3 months)		(12,000)
Taxable profits		45,000

Marking guide

			Marks
(a)	2001/02	Taxable income	1
		Reason not to use loss	2
			3
	2002/03	Use s 380	1
		Net gain	1
		Loss relief	2
		Capital losses b/f set off after trading loss	1
		Annual exemption	½
		Capital losses to c/f	½
			6
(b)	1999/00		1
	2000/01, 2001/02		2
	2002/03		3
			6
			15

Business Taxation
Mock Exam 2
(December 2001 paper)

Question Paper:	
Time allowed	**3 hours**

paper 2.3

DO NOT OPEN THIS PAPER UNTIL YOU ARE READY TO START

UNDER EXAMINATION CONDITIONS

SECTION A – BOTH questions are compulsory and MUST be attempted

58   GERONIMO LTD (12/01)

Geronimo Ltd is a UK resident company that manufacturers motorcycles. The company's summarised profit and loss account for the year ended 31 March 2003 is as follows:

	£	£
Gross profit		925,940
Operating expenses		
Bad debts (note 1)	22,360	
Depreciation	83,320	
Charitable donations (note 2)	2,850	
Professional fees (note 3)	14,900	
Patent royalties (note 4)	7,200	
Repairs and renewals (note 5)	42,310	
Other expenses (all allowable)	136,520	
		(309,460)
Operating profit		616,480
Income from investments		
Debenture interest	24,700	
Bank interest (note 7)	2,800	
Loan interest (note 8)	22,000	
Dividends (note 9)	36,000	
		85,500
		701,980
Interest payable (note 10)		(45,000)
Profit before taxation		656,980

Note 1 – Bad debts
Bad debts are as follows:

	£
Trade debts written off	20,390
Loan to employee written off	100
Increase in specific bad debt provision	6,270
Decrease in general provision for doubtful debts	(4,400)
	22,360

Note 2 – Charitable donations
Charitable donations are as follows:

	£
Donation to national charity (made under the Gift Aid scheme)	1,800
Donation to national charity (not made under the Gift Aid scheme)	100
Donation to local charity (Geronimo Ltd received free advertising in the charity's magazine)	50
Gifts to customers (food hampers costing £30 each)	900
	2,850

Note 3 – Professional fees
Professional fees are as follows:

	£
Accountancy and audit fee	4,100
Legal fees in connection with the renewal of a 20-year property lease	2,400
Legal fees in connection with the issue of a debenture loan (see note 10)	8,400
	14,900

Note 4 – Patent royalties
The figure for patent royalties payable is calculated as follows:

	£
Accrued at 1 April 2002	(1,900)
Paid 31 July 2002	5,400
Paid 31 January 2003	2,300
Accrued at 31 March 2003	1,400
	7,200

The above figures are all gross. As the patent royalties were all paid to other corporate bodies they were all paid gross. The patent royalties were paid for trade purposes.

Note 5 – Repairs and renewals
The figure of £42,310 for repairs includes £6,200 for replacing part of a wall that was knocked down by a lorry, and £12,200 for initial repairs to an office building that was acquired during the year ended 31 March 2003. The office building was not usable until the repairs were carried out, and this fact was represented by a reduced purchase price.

Note 6 – Debenture interest
The debenture interest arose in respect of a debenture in another UK company taken out for non trading purposes. Interest of £12,350 was received on 30 September 2002 and 31 March 2003 respectively. There was no accrual of debenture interest at the beginning or end of the year.

Note 7 – Bank interest received
The bank interest was received on 31 March 2003. The bank deposits are held for non-trading purposes.

Note 8 – Loan interest received
The figure for loan interest received is calculated as follows:

	£
Accrued at 1 April 2002	(5,500)
Received 30 June 2002	11,000
Received 31 December 2002	11,000
Accrued at 31 March 2003	5,500
	22,000

The above figures are all gross. The loan was made for non-trading purposes to another UK company.

Note 9 – Dividends received
The dividends were received from other UK companies. The figure of £36,000 is the actual amount received.

Note 10 – Interest payable
Geronimo Ltd raised a debenture loan on 1 July 2002. The loan was used for trading purposes. Interest of £30,000 was paid on 31 December 2002, and £15,000 was accrued at 31 March 2003. These figure are gross.

Note 11 – Plant and machinery
On 1 April 2002 the tax written down value of the general pool of plant and machinery was £52,800. There were no purchases or sales of plant and machinery during the year ended 31 March 2003.

Note 12 – Other information
Geronimo Ltd has no associated companies.

Required

(a) (i) Calculate Geronimo Ltd's tax adjusted Schedule DI profit for the year ended 31 March 2003. (11 marks)

(ii) Calculate the corporation tax payable by Geronimo Ltd for the year ended 31 March 2003. (11 marks)

(b) State the date by which Geronimo Ltd will have to file its corporation tax return for the above period, the penalties for late filing and the date by which corporation tax for the period is due. (8 marks)

(30 marks)

59 AMANDA SELLIT (12/01)

Amanda Sellit is employed by Fashionable plc as a sales manager. She has also been in part-time self-employment since 1 January 2001 running an internet café. The following information is available for 2002/03.

Self-employment

1 Her tax adjusted Schedule DI loss for the year ended 31 December 2002 is £6,700. This figure is before taking account of capital allowances.

2 The tax written down values at 31 December 2001 are as follows:

	£
General pool	17,600
Short-life asset	12,600

3 The following transactions took place during the year ended 31 December 2002:

		£
29 March	Sold the short-life asset	7,900
15 April	Sold equipment	2,600
4 May	Purchased a computer	8,200
8 May	Purchased computer software	1,400
10 June	Purchased a motor car	14,600
19 July	Purchased furniture	1,300

The equipment sold on 15 April 2002 for £2,600 originally cost £2,360. The motor car purchased on 10 June 2002 is used by Amanda, and 15% of the mileage is for business purposes.

Employment

1 Amanda is paid a salary of £42,000 pa by Fashionable plc.

2 Amanda pays an annual professional subscription of £160 to the Institute of Sales Managers.

3 Fashionable plc provides Amanda with a 1800cc motor car with a list price of £14,100. The CO_2 emissions of the car are 165g/km. The company paid for the petrol in respect of all the mileage done by Amanda during 2002/03.

4 Fashionable plc has provided Amanda with living accommodation since 1999. The property was purchased in 1988 for £90,000. Its market value when first provided to Amanda was £185,000. It has a rateable value of £7,000. The furniture in the property cost £8,000, and Fashionable plc pays for the annual running costs of £3,500. The living accommodation is not job-related.

Other information

1   Amanda pays a patent royalty of £130 (net) per month in respect of specialised computer equipment that she uses in her internet café.

2   Amanda contributes £100 (gross) per month into a personal pension scheme. She is not a member of Fashionable plc's occupational pension scheme.

Required

(a) **Calculate Amanda's Schedule DI trading loss for 2002/03.**   (9 marks)

(b) **Assuming that Amanda claims loss relief under s.380 ICTA 1988 against her total income for 2002/03, calculate her taxable income for 2002/03. The official rate of interest for 2002/03 is 5%.**   (13 marks)

(c) **Describe the alternative ways in which Amanda could have relieved her Schedule DI trading loss for 2002/03.**   (3 marks)

(25 marks)

SECTION B – THREE questions ONLY to be attempted

60   DYNAMO LTD (12/01)

Dynamo Ltd commenced trading as a wholesaler on 1 November 2002. Its sales have been as follows:

2002		£	2003		£
2002	November	3,200	2003	June	4,500
	December	2,800		July	4,300
2003	January	3,300		August	5,100
	February	4,100		September	4,900
	March	2,700		October	6,200
	April	3,700		November	5,800
	May	3,900		December	8,500

The company's sales are all standard rated, and the above figures are exclusive of VAT.

Dynamo Ltd only sells goods, and at present issues sales invoices that show (1) the invoice date and invoice number, (2) the type of supply, (3) the quantity and a description of the goods supplied, (4) Dynamo Ltd's name and address, and (5) the name and address of the customer. The company does not offer any discount for prompt payment.

Required

(a) Explain from what date Dynamo Ltd will be required to compulsorily register for VAT, and what action the company must then take.   (5 marks)

(b) Explain the circumstances in which Dynamo Ltd will be allowed to recover input VAT incurred on goods purchased and services incurred prior to the date of VAT registration.   (4 marks)

(c) State the additional information that Dynamo Ltd will have to show on its sales invoice in order that these are valid for VAT purposes.   (3 marks)

(d) Advise Dynamo Ltd of the VAT rules that determine the tax point in respect of a supply of goods.   (3 marks)

(15 marks)

61   ASTUTE LTD (12/01)

Astute Ltd sold a factory on 15 February 2003 for £320,000. The factory was purchased on 24 October 1996 for £164,000, and was extended at a cost of £37,000 during March 1998. During May 1999 the roof of the factory was replaced at a cost of £24,000 following a fire. Astute Ltd incurred legal fees of £3,600 in connection with the purchase of the factory, and legal fees of £6,200 in connection with the disposal.

Indexation factors are as follows:

October 1996 to February 2003	0.146
March 1998 to February 2003	0.096
May 1999 to February 2003	0.064

Astute Ltd is considering the following alternative ways of reinvesting the proceeds from the sale of its factory:

1   A freehold warehouse can be purchased for £340,000.
2   A freehold office building can be purchased for £275,000.
3   A leasehold factory on a 40-year lease can be acquired for a premium of £350,000.

The reinvestment will take place during May 2003. All of the above buildings have been, or will be, used for business purposes.

Required

(a) State the conditions that must be met in order that rollover relief can be claimed. You are not expected to list the categories of asset that qualify for rollover relief. (3 marks)

(b) Before taking account of any available rollover relief, calculate Astute Ltd's chargeable gain in respect of the disposal of the factory. (5 marks)

(c) Advise Astute Ltd of the rollover relief that will be available in respect of each of the three alternative reinvestments. Your answer should include details of the base cost of the replacement asset for each alternative. (7 marks)

(15 marks)

62   RED PLC (12/01)

(a) Red plc owns 100% of the ordinary share capital of Scarlet Ltd and Crimson Ltd. The results of each company for the year ended 31 March 2003 are as follows:

	Red plc £	Scarlet plc £	Crimson plc £
Tax adjusted Schedule DI profit/(loss)	900,000	210,000	(140,000)
Schedule A	-	10,000	30,000

As at 31 March 2003 Scarlet Ltd and Crimson Ltd has unused trading losses of £15,000 and £20,000 respectively. Red plc has no other associated companies.

Required

Assuming that reliefs are claimed in the most favourable manner, calculate the corporation tax liabilities of Red plc, Scarlet Ltd and Crimson Ltd for the year ended 31 March 2003. (8 marks)

(b) White plc owns 100% of the ordinary share capital of Cream Ltd. For the year ended 31 March 2003 White plc pays corporation tax at the rate of 30% and Cream Ltd pays corporation tax at the rate of 19%.

On 15 August 2002 White plc sold an office building, and this resulted in a capital gain of £110,000. On 20 February 2003 Cream Ltd sold a factory, and this resulted in a capital loss of £35,000.

As at 31 March 2003 Cream Ltd has unused capital losses of £40,000.

Required

State the time limit for White plc and Cream Ltd to make a joint election so that Cream Ltd is treated as disposing of White plc's office building, and explain why such an election will be beneficial. (3 marks)

(c) Blue plc owns 85% of the ordinary share capital of Azure Ltd and 45% of the ordinary share capital of Violet Ltd. Azure Ltd owns 85% of Green Ltd. Blue plc makes a Schedule D Case I loss.

Required

State, giving appropriate reasons, to which companies Blue plc can surrender its loss of £200,000 and to which companies Blue plc can make no gain/no loss transfers or capital assets. (4 marks)

(15 marks)

63   ABDUL PATEL (12/01)

Abdul Patel is to commence in business on 1 April 2002 running a retail shop (you should assume that today's date is 15 March 2002).

His tax adjusted Schedule DI profit for the year ended 31 March 2003 is expected to be £80,000.

Abdul is unsure whether he should run his business as a sole trader or via a limited company. If the business is run as a limited company it will be called AP Ltd, and Abdul will personally withdraw £45,000 of the company's profits. This will be either as:

1   Director's remuneration (the gross remuneration will be £45,000), or
2   Dividends (the figure actually withdrawn will be £45,000).

The following information is also available:

1   For 2002/03 Abdul's investment income will fully utilise his personal allowance and 10% tax band, and partly utilise the basic rate tax band.

2   Abdul will have £25,000 of the basic rate tax band unused for 2002/03.

Required

(a)   **Calculate Abdul's liability to income tax, Class 2 NIC and Class 4 NIC for 2002/03 if he runs his business as a sole trader. You are not expected to calculate the tax liability on Abdul's investment income.**   (3 marks)

(b)   **Assuming that Abdul incorporates his business on 1 April 2002, calculate the corporation tax liability of AP Ltd for the year ended 31 March 2003 and the income tax and Class 1 NIC liability of Abdul for 2002/03 if he withdraws:**

    (i)   **Gross director's remuneration of £45,000, or**   (8 marks)
    (ii)   **Net dividends of £45,000.** No NI .   (4 marks)

You are not expected to calculate the tax liability on Abdul's investment income.

(15 marks)

64   RUBY CHAN (12/01)

Ruby Chan has been a self-employed computer consultant since 1991. Her income for 2002/03 is as follows:

	£
Tax adjusted Schedule DII profit	26,700
Schedule A profit	3,300
Building society interest (net)	5,200
Capital gain	12,400

The capital gain is after taking account of indexation and taper relief.

Ruby's payments on account for 2002/03 totalled £3,280.

Required

(a)   (i)   **Calculate the income tax, Class 4 NIC and CGT payable by Ruby for 2002/03.**   (8 marks)

    (ii)   **Calculate Ruby's balancing payment for 2002/03, and her payments on account for 2002/03. Your answer should include the relevant due dates.**   (2 marks)

(b) **Advise Ruby of the consequences of:**

(i) **Not filing her self-assessment tax return for 2002/03 until 31 May 2004.**

(2 marks)

(ii) **Not making the balancing payment for 2002/03 until 31 May 2004. The rate of interest on unpaid tax for 2002/03 is 6.5%.** (3 marks)

(15 marks)

MOCK EXAM 2 (DECEMBER 2001 PAPER): ANSWERS

DO NOT TURN THIS PAGE UNTIL YOU
HAVE COMPLETED THE MOCK EXAM

143

WARNING! APPLYING OUR MARKING SCHEME

If you decide to mark your paper using our marking scheme, you should bear in mind the following points.

1   The BPP solutions are not definitive: you will see that we have applied the marking scheme to our solutions to show how good answers should gain marks, but there may be more than one way to answer the question. You must try to judge fairly whether different points made in your answers are correct and relevant and therefore worth marks according to our marking scheme.

2   If you have a friend or colleague who is studying or has studied this paper, you might ask him or her to mark your paper for you, thus gaining a more objective assessment. Remember you and your friend are not trained or objective markers, so try to avoid complacency or pessimism if you appear to have done very well or very badly.

3   You should be aware that BPP's answers are longer than you would be expected to write. Sometimes, therefore, you would gain the same number of marks for making the basic point as we have shown as being available for a slightly more detailed or extensive solution.

It is most important that you analyse your solutions in detail and that you attempt to be as objective as possible.

A PLAN OF ATTACK

What's the worst thing you could be doing right now if this was the actual exam paper? Sharpening your pencil? Wondering how to celebrate the end of the exam in 2 hours 59 minutes time? Panicking, flapping and generally getting in a right old state?

Well, they're all pretty bad, so turn back to the paper and let's sort out a **plan of attack**!

First things first

Spend a good 5 minutes looking through the paper in detail working out which optional questions to do and the order in which to attack the questions. You've then got **two options**.

Option 1 (if you're thinking 'Help!')

If you're a bit worried about the paper, do the questions in the order of how well you think you can answer them. You will probably find the optional questions in Section B less daunting than the compulsory questions in Section A so start with Section B.

- If you are totally happy with chargeable gains calculations then start with **question 61**. If you feel you are doing these computations correctly, it will boost your confidence. If you particularly like computations, you could start with part (b) of the question. Allow yourself 27 minutes to answer the question but make sure that you don't spend too long on part (b) (10 minutes at the most) – you need to leave 5 minutes for part (a) and 12 minutes for part (c).

- **Question 63** covers trading as a sole trader or company and NICs. If you feel confident in this area, this question was worth attempting.

- **Question 64** covers income tax self assessment.

- If you like VAT, **question 60** was worth attempting. **Question 62** was a fairly standard groups question that should have given you no trouble if you like groups.

- The requirements of all of the **questions** are broken down. This should help you allocate your time.

When you've spent the allocated time on the three questions in Section B turn to the compulsory questions in Section A. You should have 1 hour and 30 minutes left at this point in the exam. Read the compulsory questions through thoroughly before you launch into them. Once you start make sure you allocate your time to the parts within the questions according to the marks available and that, where possible, you attempt the easy marks first.

Lastly, what you mustn't forget is that you have to **answer both questions in Section A, and THREE questions from Section B**. Once you've decided on your three questions from Section B, it might be worth putting a line through the other questions so that you are not tempted to answer them!

Option 2 (if you're thinking 'It's a doddle')

It never pays to be over confident but if you're not quaking in your shoes about the exam then **turn straight to the compulsory questions** in Section A. You've got to do them so you might as well get them over and done with.

Once you've done the compulsory questions, choose three of the questions in Section B.

Your choice from the other questions really depends on what you are most confident at. They are all fairly standard questions.

No matter how many times we remind you....

Always, always **allocate your time** according to the marks for the question in total and then according to the parts of the question. And **always, always follow the requirements** exactly. In Question 63, for example, you were told not to calculate the tax liability on Abdul's investment income – so you shouldn't have done so. Its a waste of time and attracts no marks.

You've got spare time at the end of the exam.....?

If you have allocated your time properly then you **shouldn't have time on your hands** at the end of the exam. But if you find yourself with five or ten minutes to spare, check over your work to make sure that there are no silly arithmetical errors.

Forget about it!

And don't worry if you found the paper difficult. More than likely other candidates will too. If this were the real thing you would need to **forget** the exam the minute you leave the exam hall and **think about the next one**. Or, if it's the last one, **celebrate**!

58   GERONIMO LTD

> **Pass marks**. Although they are provided in the answer for tutorial purposes, detailed explanations to support the Schedule D Case I profit adjustments were not required. The requirement asked for calculations.

(a)   (i)   Schedule D Case I profit

	£	£
Profit per accounts		656,980
Add:		
Loan to employee	100	
Written off depreciation	83,320	
Gift Aid donation	1,800	
Gift to national charity	100	
Gifts to customers	900	
Repairs	12,200	
		98,420
Less:		
Debenture interest	24,700	
Bad debt provision	4,400	
Bank interest	2,800	
Loan interest	22,000	
Dividends	36,000	
Capital allowances (W1)	13,200	
		(103,100)
		652,300

Tutorial notes

1   The costs of renewing a short lease and of obtaining loan finance for trading purposes are allowable.

2   The replacement of the wall is allowable since the whole structure is not being replaced. The repairs to the office building are not allowable, being capital in nature, as the building was not in a usable state when purchased and this was reflected in the purchase price.

3   The patent royalties were paid for trade purposes so the amount charged in the accounts is deductible for Schedule D Case I purposes.

4   The debenture interest paid has been deducted in arriving at the accounts profit. As the loan was raised for trading purposes, no adjustment to the Schedule D Case I profit is required.

(b)

	£
Schedule D Case I	652,300
Schedule D Case III (£24,700 + £2,800 + £22,000)	49,500
Less: gift aid donation	(1,800)
Profits chargeable to corporation tax	700,000
FII (£36,000 × $\frac{100}{90}$)	40,000
'Profits'	740,000
Corporation tax	
£700,000 × 30%	210,000
Less:	
11/400 (1,500,000 – 740,000) × $\frac{700,000}{740,000}$	(19,770)
Corporation tax payable	190,230

(b) The corporation tax return for the year to 31 March 2003 must be filed by 31 March 2004.

The initial penalty for late filing is £100, rising to £200 if the return is more than 3 months late. If each of the two previous returns were late these penalties rise to £500 and £1,000 respectively. An additional tax geared penalty is applied if a return is more than 6 months late. The penalty is 10% of the tax unpaid 6 months after the return was due if the total delay up to 12 months, and 20% of that tax if the return is over 12 months late.

Geronimo Ltd is not a large company so the corporation tax of £190,230 is due on 1 January 2004.

Workings

1 Capital allowances

	£
TWDV b/f	52,800
WDA @ 25%	(13,200)
	39,600

Marking guide		Marks
(a)	Profit before tax	1
	Depreciation	1
	Bad debts	1
	Donations and gifts	2
	Professional fees	1
	Patent royalties	1
	Repairs	1
	Interest payable	1
	Capital allowances	1
		11
	Corporation tax computation	
	Schedule DI	1
	Schedule DIII - Bank interest	1
	- Loan interest	1
	Debenture interest accrued	2
	Charges on income - Gift Aid donation	1
	Franked investment income	1
	Corporation tax	2
		11
(b)	Return due date	1
	£100 penalty	1
	£200 penalty	1
	£500 penalty	1
	£1,000 penalty	1
	10% penalty	1
	20% penalty	1
	Tax due date	1
		8
		30

59   AMANDA SELLIT

> **Pass marks.** (i) As the property was purchased more than 6 years before it was provided, the market value of £185,000 must be used in computing the additional accommodation benefit.
>
> (ii) The personal pension contributions do not reduce taxable income. Instead they are paid net of basic rate tax and additional tax relief is given by extending the basic rate band.

(a)

	£
Loss	6,700
Capital allowances (W1)	19,080
Schedule D Case I loss	25,780

(b)

	Non-savings income £
Schedule E (W2)	64,405
Less: patent royalty	(2,000)
	62,405
Less: s 380 relief	(25,780)
	36,625
Less: personal allowances	(4,615)
Taxable income	32,010

(c)   The Schedule DI loss for 2002/03 could alternatively have been:

   (i)   Relieved against STI under s380 ICTA 1988 in 2001/02.

   (ii) Relieved against STI under s381 ICTA 1988 in 1999/00, 2000/01 and 2001/02 on a FIFO basis.

   (iii) Relieved under s385 ICTA 1988 against future profits of the same trade.

Workings

1   Capital allowances

	FYA £	Pool £	Short life asset £	Private use £	Allowances £
TWDV b/f		17,600	12,600		
Addition				14,600	
Disposals		(2,360)	(7,900)		
		15,240	4,700	14,600	
WDA @ 25%/restricted		(3,810)		(3,000) (15%)	4,260
Balancing allowance					
Furniture	1,300		(4,700)		4,700
FYA @ 40%	(520)				520
		780			
Computer	8,200				
Computer software	1,400				
	9,600				
FYA @ 100%	(9,600)				9,600
		12,210	-	11,600	
					19,080

Note. Amanda's business qualifies as a small enterprise for capital allowance purposes. This means that FYA are available at 100% on the computer equipment.

2   Schedule E

	£
Salary	42,000
Subscription	(160)
Car (£14,100 × 15%) (Note)	2,115
Fuel	2,850
Rateable value	7,000
Additional accommodation benefit (£185,000 − £75,000) × 5%	5,500
Running costs	3,500
Furniture (£8,000 × 20%)	1,600
Schedule E	64,405

Note. As the CO_2 emissions of the car are 165g/km the taxable car % is 15%.

Marking guide		Marks
(a)	Schedule DI loss	1
	Capital allowances - Pool	2½
	- FYAs	2½
	- Motor car	1½
	- Short-life asset	1½
		9
(b)	Salary	½
	Car benefit	2
	Fuel benefit	1
	Living accommodation - Rateable value	½
	- Additional benefit	2
	- Furniture	1
	- Running costs	½
	Professional subscription	1
	Personal pension contributions (not deducted)	1
	Charge on income	2
	Loss relief	1
	Personal allowance	½
		13
(c)	S 380 ICTA 1988	1
	S 381 ICTA 1988	1
	S 385 ICTA 1988	1
		3
		25

60   DYNAMO LTD

Pass marks. To score well you would need to have answered all four parts of this question. It was important to ensure that you allocated your time carefully between all four parts.

(a) Dynamo Ltd will be required to **compulsorily register for VAT when its taxable supplies in any 12 month period exceed £55,000**.

This will happen on 31 December 2003 when the value of taxable supplies will amount to £57,000.

Dynamo Ltd will have to **notify C&E of its need to register within 30 days,** ie by 30 January 2004. The company will be registered from 1 February 2004, or from an agreed earlier date.

(b) VAT incurred on goods purchased prior to registration can be reclaimed if:

   (i)   The goods were acquired for the purposes of a business which either was carried on or was to be carried on at the time of supply.

   (ii)   The goods have not been supplied onwards or consumed before the date of registration (although they may have been used to make other goods which are still held).

   (iii) The VAT must have been incurred in the three years prior to the effective date of registration.

   VAT incurred on the supply of services prior to registration can be reclaimed if:

   (i)   The services were supplied for the purposes of a business which either was or was to be carried on at the time of supply.

   (ii)   The services were supplied within six months prior to the date of registration.

(c) The following additional information is needed for the invoices to be valid for VAT purposes:

   (i)   Dynamo Ltd's **VAT registration number**.

   (ii)   The **tax point**.

   (iii) The **rate of VAT** for each supply.

   (iv)   The **VAT exclusive amount** for each supply.

   (v)   The **total invoice price excluding VAT**.

   (vi)   **Each VAT rate applicable, the amount of VAT at each rate and the total amount of VAT**.

(d) For a supply of goods, **the basic tax point is the date goods are removed or made available to the customer.**

   If **an invoice is issued** or **payment is received before the basic tax point, then this becomes the actual tax point.**

   If **an invoice is issued in the 14 days following the basic tax point, the invoice date normally becomes the actual tax point.**

Marking guide		Marks
(a)	Registration limit	1
	December 2003	2
	Notification	1
	Date of registration	1
		5
(b)	Goods	
	Business purposes/not sold or consumed	1
	Three years	1
	Services	
	Business purposes	1
	Six months	1
		4
(c)	The VAT registration number	½
	The tax point	½
	The rate of VAT for each supply	½
	The VAT-exclusive amount for each supply	½
	The total VAT-exclusive amount	½
	The amount of VAT payable	½
		3
(d)	Basic tax point	1
	Payment received or invoice issued	1
	Issue of invoice within 14 days	1
		3
		15

61   ASTUTE LTD

Pass marks. When this question was set the examiner said there was little awareness of the reinvestment period and that the reinvestment in the depreciating asset caused problems.

(a) For rollover relief to be available:

(i) A new asset must be acquired **in the period commencing 12 months before and ending 3 years after the disposal.**

(ii) Both **the old and the new assets must be used for trade purposes and must be on the list of qualifying assets.**

(iii) The new asset must **immediately be brought into trade use.**

(b)

		£
Disposal proceeds		320,000
Less:	Cost	(164,000)
	Legal fees on purchase	(3,600)
	Extension	(37,000)
	Legal fees on sale	(6,200)
	Gain	109,200
	Less: Indexation	
	(£164,000 + 3,600) × 0.146	(24,470)
	£37,000 × 0.096	(3,552)
	Chargeable gain	81,178

Note 1

Enhancement expenditure reflected in the state or nature of an asset at the date of disposal can be deducted in computing a chargeable gain.

The factory extension is enhancement expenditure as it has added to the value of the factory.

The replacement of the roof is a repair, not enhancement expenditure, so the cost is not deductible.

(c) (i) Purchase of a warehouse.
All proceeds are reinvested.
∴ gain rolled over – £81,178
Base cost of warehouse
£340,000 – £81,178 = £258,822

(ii) Freehold office building £275,000
Proceeds not reinvested = £45,000
Gain rolled over =
£81,178 – £45,000 = £36,178
Base cost of building
£275,000 – £36,178 = £238,822

(iii) Leasehold Factory
Proceeds fully reinvested
∴ Gain deferred = £81,178

The factory is a depreciating asset. This means that the base cost of the factory is not adjusted. It is £350,000. The gain is merely deferred until the earliest of 10 years from the date of acquisition or the date the leasehold factory is disposed of or the date it ceases to be used in the trade.

Marking guide	Marks	
(a) Period of reinvestment	1	
Qualifying assets	1	
Brought into business use	1	
		3
(b) Net sale proceeds	1	
Deductions	2	
Indexation	2	
		5
(c) Freehold warehouse		
Rollover relief	1	
Base cost	1	
Freehold office building		
Amount not rolled over	1	
Base cost	1	
Leasehold factory		
Deferral relief	1	
Depreciating asset	1	
10 years/date of sale/not used intrade	1	
		7
		15

62   RED PLC

> **Pass marks.** Brought forward trading losses cannot be group relieved. A mark was given for the loss carry forward even if not explicitly stated.

(a)

	Red plc £	Scarlet Ltd £	Crimson Ltd £
Schedule DI	900,000	210,000	-
Less: Loss b/f	-	(15,000)	
Schedule A		10,000	30,000
	900,000	205,000	30,000
Less: group relief	(35,000)	(105,000)	
Profits chargeable to corporation tax	865,000	100,000	30,000
CT @ 30%	259,500		
CT @ 19%		19,000	5,700

Workings

There are three associated companies so the lower and upper limits for small companies' rate purposes are £100,000 and £500,000 respectively. Crimson Ltd's current period loss is therefore initially surrendered to Scarlet Ltd to bring PCTCT down to £100,000. The balance is then surrendered to Red plc, where it saves tax at the marginal rate of 30%.

It is not possible to surrender brought forward losses, so Crimson Ltd's brought forward loss of £20,000 must be carried forward to future accounting periods. It cannot be set off against the Sch A income as the Schedule A income is not trading income. The limits for the starting rate are £3,333 and £16,667 respectively, so the Sch A income is taxable at the small companies' rate.

(b) The **time limit for the election is 2 years from the end of the accounting period.** This means that White plc and Cream Ltd must make the election by 31 March 2005.

The election will be beneficial as Cream Ltd will then be able to set both its brought forward capital loss and its current period capital loss against the gain arising. This will leave a net gain of £35,000 to be taxed in Cream Ltd. It is beneficial for the gain remaining to be taxed in Cream Ltd as Cream Ltd suffers a lower rate of corporation tax than White plc.

(c) **Blue plc may surrender its losses to Azure Ltd.**

Violet Ltd is a 45% subsidiary of Blue plc and Green Ltd is a 72.25% (85% × 85%) subsidiary. As **neither of these companies is 75% owned, Blue plc may not surrender losses to either of them**.

Blue Ltd may make no gain/loss transfers for chargeable gains purposes to both Azure Ltd and Green Ltd. Green Ltd is in the capital gains group as it is at least 75% owned by Azure Ltd and Blue plc has an effective interest of more than 50%.

Marking guide		Marks
(a)	Schedule DI	1
	Loss relief s 393(1)	1
	Schedule A	1
	Associated companies	1
	Group relief	2
	Corporation tax	1
	Trading loss carried forward	1
		8
(b)	Time limit	1
	Set off of capital losses	1
	Tax rate	1
		3
(c)	Group relief	2
	Captial gains group	2
		4
		15

63   ABDUL PATEL

Pass marks. It was important not to ignore the fact that only £25,000 of the basic rate band was available. This approach was used by the examiner to simplify the repetitive income tax calculations.

(a)   Class 2 NICs

$£2 \times 52 = £104$

Class 4 NICs

$7\% \times (£30,420 - £4,615) = £1,806$

	£
Income tax	
$£25,000 \times 22\%$	5,500
$£55,000 \times 40\%$	22,000
Income tax liability	27,500

(b)   (i)

CT Liability

	£
Profits	80,000
Remuneration	(45,000)
Class 1 NICs	
$(£45,000 - £4,615) \times 11.8\%$	(4,765)
	30,235

	£
CT @ 19%	5,745
Less 19/400 (50,000 − 30,235)	(939)
	4,806

Abdul's income tax liability:

	£
$£25,000 \times 22\%$	5,500
$£20,000 \times 40\%$	8,000
	13,500

Abdul's Class 1 NICs:

$(£30,420 - £4,615) \times 10\% = £2,580$

(ii)   Dividends £45,000

CT liability

£80,000 × 19% = £15,200

Abdul's income tax liability

Dividends £45,000 × $\frac{100}{90}$ = £50,000

	£
£25,000 × 10%	2,500
£25,000 32.5%	8,125
	10,625
Less: tax credit on dividends	(5,000)
	5,625

Marking guide		Marks
(a)	Income tax liability	1
	Class 2 NIC	1
	Class 4 NIC	1
		3
(b)	Director's remuneration	
	Employer Class 1 NIC	2
	Corporation tax - PCTCT	1½
	- Liability	1½
	Income tax liability	1
	Employee Class 1 NIC	2
		8
	Dividends	
	Corporation tax liability	1
	Income tax - Gross dividends	1
	- Liability	2
		4
		15

64   RUBY CHAN

> **Pass marks.** The examiner did not penalise candidates for a poor layout, but a poor layout did result in problems when calculating the balancing payment and payments on account.

(a)

	Non-savings income	Savings (excl. dividend income)	Total
	£	£	£
Schedule D Case II	26,700		
Schedule A	3,300		
Building society interest (× 100/80)		6,500	
	30,000	6,500	36,500
Less: Personal allowance	(4,615)		
	25,385	6,500	31,885

	£
Tax on non-savings income	
£1,920 × 10%	192
£23,465 × 22%	5,162
Tax on savings income	
£4,515 × 20%	903
£1,985 × 40%	794
	7,051
Less: tax suffered	(1,300)
Income tax payable	5,751

Class 4 NICs payable	
(£26,700 − 4,615) × 7%	£1,546

	£
Capital gain	12,400
Less: Annual exemption	(7,700)
Capital gain	4,700
CGT @ 40% = £1,880	
Total Class 4 NIC and income tax (£5,751 + £1,546)	7,297
Less: Payments on account	(3,280)
Balancing payment of income tax and NICs due 31.1.04	4,017

All of the CGT is due 31.1.04

Payments on account for 2003/04:

£7,297 × $\frac{1}{2}$ = £3,649.

These are due on 31.1.04 and 31.7.04.

No payments on account of CGT are due.

(b) If Ruby's income tax return is filed on 31.5.04 there will be a fixed penalty of £100. In addition it would be possible for a daily penalty of £60 to be charged.

(c) Interest of 6.5% will be charged on the late paid balancing payment from 31.1.04 to 31.5.04.

ie interest of $\frac{4}{12}$ × 6.5% × £4,017 = £87 is due.

In addition as the balancing payment was not made within 28 days of the due date a 5% surcharge of £201 will be imposed.

Marking guide		Marks	
(a)	Taxable income	2	
	Income tax	2	
	Tax suffered at source	1	
	Class 4 NIC	1	
	CGT	2	
	Balancing payment	1	
	Payments on account	1	
			10
(b)	Self-assessment tax return		
	Fixed penalty	1	
	Daily penalty	1	
	Balancing payment		
	Interest	1	
	Calculation	1	
	Surcharge	1	
			5
			15

TAX RATES AND ALLOWANCES

A   INCOME TAX

1   Rates

	2001/02 £	%	2002/03 £	%
Starting rate	1 - 1,880	10	1 - 1,920	10
Basic rate	1,881 - 29,400	22	1,921 - 29,900	22
Higher rate	29,401 and above	40	29,901 and above	40

Savings (excl. Dividend) income is taxed at 20% if it falls in the basic rate band. Dividend income in both the starting rate and the basic rate bands is taxed at 10%. Dividend income within the higher rate band is taxed at 32.5%.

2   Allowances

	2001/02 £	2002/03 £
Personal allowance	4,535	4,615

3   Cars – taxable percentage 2002/03

The taxable percentage is 15% for petrol engined cars with a baseline CO_2 emissions figure of 165g/km or less.

4   Car fuel scale charges

	2002/03 Petrol £	Diesel £
Cars having a cylinder capacity		
1,400 cc or less	2,240	2,850
1,401 cc to 2,000 cc	2,850	2,850
More than 2,000 cc	4,200	4,200
Cars not having a cylinder capacity	4,200	4,200

5   Authorised mileage rates (AMR)- 2002/03 rates

The rates for the maximum tax free mileage allowances for 2002/03 are as follows:

Car mileage rates

First 10,000 miles	40p per mile
Over 10,000 miles	25p per mile

Bicycles	*Motor cycles*
20p per mile	24p per mile

6   *Personal pension contribution limits*

(handwritten note: age at start of fiscal year)

Age	Maximum percentage %
Up to 35	17.5
36 – 45	20.0
46 – 50	25.0
51 – 55	30.0
56 – 60	35.0
61 or more	40.0

Subject to earnings cap of £95,400 for 2001/02 and £97,200 for 2002/03.

7   *Capital allowances*

	%
Plant and machinery	
Writing down allowance*	25
First year allowance (acquisitions 2.7.97 - 1.7.98)**	50
First year allowance (acquisitions after 2.7.98)	40
First year allowance (information and communication technology equipment - period 1.4.00 - 31.3.03, energy saving equipment, flats above shops)	100
Industrial buildings allowance	
Writing down allowance: post 5.11.62	4
pre 6.11.62	2

* 6% reducing balance for certain long life assets.

** 12% for certain long life assets.

B   CORPORATION TAX

1   *Rates*

Financial Year	2000	2001	2002
Starting rate	10%	10%	0%
Small companies' rate	20%	20%	19%
Full rate	30%	30%	30%
	£	£	£
Starting rate lower limit	10,000	10,000	10,000
Starting rate upper limit	50,000	50,000	50,000
Lower limit	300,000	300,000	300,000
Upper limit	1,500,000	1,500,000	1,500,000
Taper relief fraction			
Starting rate	1/40	1/40	19/400
Small companies' rate	1/40	1/40	11/400

2   *Marginal relief*

$(M - P) \times I/P \times \text{Marginal relief fraction}$

C   VALUE ADDED TAX

1   *Registration and deregistration limits*

	To 24.4.02	From 25.4.02
Registration limit	£54,000	£55,000
Deregistration limit	£52,000	£53,000

2   *Scale charges for private motoring*

For the first accounting period beginning after 1 May 2002 (VAT inclusive)

	Quarterly	
	Petrol	Diesel
Up to 1400 cc	226	212
1401 to 2000 cc	286	212
Over 2000cc	422	268

D   RATES OF INTEREST

Official rate of interest: 5% (assumed)

Rate of interest on unpaid/tax: 6.5% (assumed)

Rate of interest on overpaid tax: 2.5% (assumed)

E   CAPITAL GAINS TAX

1   *Retail prices index (January 1987 = 100.0)*

	1982	1983	1984	1985	1986	1987	1988	1989	1990	1991
Jan		82.6	86.8	91.2	96.2	100.0	103.3	111.0	119.5	130.2
Feb		83.0	87.2	91.9	96.6	100.4	103.7	111.8	120.2	130.9
Mar	79.4	83.1	87.5	92.8	96.7	100.6	104.1	112.3	121.4	131.4
Apr	81.0	84.3	88.6	94.8	97.7	101.8	105.8	114.3	125.1	133.1
May	81.6	84.6	89.0	95.2	97.8	101.9	106.2	115.0	126.2	133.5
Jun	81.9	84.8	89.2	95.4	97.8	101.9	106.6	115.4	126.7	134.1
Jul	81.9	85.3	89.1	95.2	97.5	101.8	106.7	115.5	126.8	133.8
Aug	81.9	85.7	89.9	95.5	97.8	102.1	107.9	115.8	128.1	134.1
Sept	81.9	86.1	90.1	95.4	98.3	102.4	108.4	116.6	129.3	134.6
Oct	82.3	86.4	90.7	95.6	98.5	102.9	109.5	117.5	130.3	135.1
Nov	82.7	86.7	91.0	95.9	99.3	103.4	110.0	118.5	130.0	135.6
Dec	82.5	86.9	90.9	96.0	99.6	103.3	110.3	118.8	129.9	135.7

	1992	1993	1994	1995	1996	1997	1998	1999	2000	2001	2002*	2003*
Jan	135.6	137.9	141.3	146.0	150.2	154.4	159.5	163.4	166.6	171.1	173.6	176.0
Feb	136.3	138.8	142.1	146.9	150.9	155.0	160.3	163.7	167.5	172.0	173.8	176.2
Mar	136.7	139.3	142.5	147.5	151.5	154.4	160.8	164.1	168.4	172.2	174.0	176.4
Apr	138.8	140.6	144.2	149.0	152.6	156.3	162.6	165.2	170.1	173.1	174.2	176.6
May	139.3	141.1	144.7	149.6	152.9	156.9	163.5	165.6	170.7	174.2	174.4	176.8
Jun	139.3	141.0	144.7	149.8	153.0	157.5	163.4	165.6	171.1	174.4	174.6	177.0
Jul	138.8	140.7	144.0	149.1	152.4	157.5	163.0	165.1	170.5	173.3	174.8	177.2
Aug	138.9	141.3	144.7	149.9	153.1	158.5	163.7	165.5	170.5	174.0	175.0	177.4
Sept	139.4	141.9	145.0	150.6	153.8	159.3	164.4	166.2	171.7	174.6	175.2	177.6
Oct	139.9	141.8	145.2	149.8	153.8	159.6	164.5	166.5	171.6	174.3	175.4	177.8
Nov	139.7	141.6	145.3	149.8	153.9	159.6	164.4	166.7	172.1	173.6	175.6	178.0
Dec	139.2	141.9	146.0	150.7	154.4	160.0	164.4	167.3	172.2	173.4	175.8	178.2

★   Estimated figures.

2   *Annual exemption (individuals)*

	£
2000/01	7,200
2001/02	7,500
2002/03	7,700

3   *Taper relief: Disposals after 6 April 2002*

Complete years after 5.4.98 for which asset held	*Business assets % of gain chargeable*	*Non business assets % of gain chargeable*
1	50 %	100 %
2	25 %	100 %
3	25 %	95 %
4	25 %	90 %
5	25 %	85 %

F   NATIONAL INSURANCE (NOT CONTRACTED OUT RATES) 2002/03

Class 1 contributions

£

Employee

Earnings threshold	4,615 (£89 pw)
Upper earnings limit (UEL)	30,420 (£585 pw)

Employer

Earnings threshold	4,615 (£89 pw)
Employee contributions	10% on earnings between the earnings threshold and the UEL
Employer contributions	11.8% on earnings above earnings threshold

Class 1A contributions

Rate 11.8%

Class 2 contributions

Rate	£2.00 pw
Small earnings exception	£4,025 pa

Class 4 contributions

Rate	7%
Lower earnings limit	£4,615
Upper earnings limit	£30,420

See overleaf for information on other
BPP products and how to order

ACCA Order

To BPP Publishing Ltd, Aldine Place, London W12 8AW
Tel: 020 8740 2211 Fax: 020 8740 1184
email: publishing@bpp.com online: www.bpp.com

Mr/Mrs/Ms (Full name) _____

Daytime delivery address _____

Postcode _____

Daytime Tel _____ Date of exam (month/year) _____

	6/02 Texts	1/03 Kits	1/03 Passcards	MCQ Cards	Tapes	Videos	7/02 i-Learn	7/02 i-Pass	Virtual Campus
PART 1									
1.1 Preparing Financial Statements	£20.95	£10.95	£6.95	£5.95	£12.95	£25.00	£34.95	£24.95	£90.00
1.2 Financial Information for Management	£20.95	£10.95	£6.95	£5.95		£25.00	£34.95	£24.95	£90.00
1.3 Managing people	£20.95	£10.95	£6.95	£5.95	£12.95	£25.00	£34.95	£24.95	£90.00
PART 2									
2.1 Information Systems	£20.95	£10.95	£6.95		£12.95	£25.00	£34.95	£24.95	£90.00
2.2 Corporate and Business Law	£20.95	£10.95	£6.95		£12.95	£25.00	£34.95	£24.95	£90.00
2.3 Business Taxation FA 2002 (for 2003 exams)†	£20.95	£10.95	£6.95		£12.95	£25.00	£34.95	£24.95	£90.00
2.4 Financial Management and Control	£20.95	£10.95	£6.95		£12.95	£25.00	£34.95	£24.95	£90.00
2.5 Financial Reporting	£20.95	£10.95	£6.95		£12.95	£25.00	£34.95	£24.95	£90.00
2.6 Audit and Internal Review	£20.95	£10.95	£6.95		£12.95	£25.00	£34.95	£24.95	£90.00
PART 3									
3.1 Audit and Assurance Services	£20.95	£10.95	£6.95		£12.95	£25.00			
3.2 Advanced Taxation FA 2002 (for 2003 exams)†	£20.95	£10.95	£6.95		£12.95	£25.00			
3.3 Performance Management	£20.95	£10.95	£6.95		£12.95	£25.00			
3.4 Business Information Management	£20.95	£10.95	£6.95		£12.95	£25.00			
3.5 Strategic Business Planning and Development	£20.95	£10.95	£6.95		£12.95	£25.00			
3.6 Advanced Corporate Reporting (7/02)	£20.95	£10.95	£6.95		£12.95	£25.00			
3.7 Strategic Financial Management	£20.95	£10.95	£6.95		£12.95	£25.00			
INTERNATIONAL STREAM									
1.1 Preparing Financial Statements	£20.95	£10.95	£6.95	£5.95					
2.5 Financial Reporting	£20.95	£10.95	£6.95						
2.6 Audit and Internal Review	£20.95	£10.95	£6.95						
3.1 Audit and Assurance Services	£20.95	£10.95	£6.95						
3.6 Advance Corporate Reporting	£20.95	£10.95	£6.95						
Success in your Research and Analysis Project – Tutorial Text (8/02)	£19.95								
Learning to Learn (7/02)	£9.95								

Subtotal £ _____

POSTAGE & PACKING

Texts/Kits

	Mail Order First	Each extra	On-line per item
UK	£5.00	£2.00	£2.00
Europe*	£6.00	£4.00	£4.00
Rest of world	£20.00	£10.00	£10.00

£ ____

Kits/Passcards/Success Tapes

	Mail Order First	Each extra	On-line per-item
UK	£2.00	£1.00	£1.00
Europe*	£2.00	£2.00	£2.00
Rest of world	£8.00	£8.00	£8.00

£ ____

Breakthrough Videos

	Mail Order First	Each extra	On-line per-item
UK	£2.00	£1.00	£1.00
Europe*	£3.00	£2.00	£2.00
Rest of world	£8.00	£8.00	£8.00

£ ____

Grand Total (incl. Postage) **£** ____

I enclose a cheque for (Cheques to *BPP Publishing*)

Or charge to Visa/Mastercard/Switch

Card Number _____

Expiry date _____ Start Date _____

Issue Number (Switch Only) _____

Signature _____

We aim to deliver to all UK addressess inside 5 working days; a signature will be required. Orders to all EU addresses should be delivered within 6 working days. All other orders to overseas addresses should be delivered within 8 working days.

* Europe includes the Republic of Ireland and the Channel Islands. † Available on the following dates: Texts 9/02, Kits 1/03, Passcards 1/03.

REVIEW FORM & FREE PRIZE DRAW

All original review forms from the entire BPP range, completed with genuine comments, will be entered into one of two draws 31 July 2003 and 31 January 2004. The names on the first four forms picked out on each occasion will be sent a cheque for £50.

Name: _____   Address: _____
_____
_____

How have you used this Kit?
(Tick one box only)

☐ Self study (book only)

☐ On a course: college (please state)_____
_____

☐ With 'correspondence' package

☐ Other _____

Why did you decide to purchase this Kit? *(Tick one box only)*

☐ Have used the complementary Study Text

☐ Have used other BPP products in the past

☐ Recommendation by friend/colleague

☐ Recommendation by a lecturer at college

☐ Saw advertising in journals

☐ Saw website

☐ Other _____

During the past six months do you recall seeing/receiving any of the following?
(Tick as many boxes as are relevant)

☐ Our advertisement in *Student Accountant*

☐ Our advertisement in *Pass*

☐ Our brochure with a letter through the post

☐ Our website

Which (if any) aspects of our advertising do you find useful?
(Tick as many boxes as are relevant)

☐ Prices and publication dates of new editions

☐ Information on product content

☐ Facility to order books off-the-page

☐ None of the above

When did you sit the exam? _____

Which BPP products have you used?

Text	☐	MCQ cards	☐	i-Learn	☐
Kit	☑	Tape	☐	i-Pass	☐
Passcard	☐	Video	☐	Virtual Campus	☐

Your ratings, comments and suggestions would be appreciated on the following areas of this Kit.

	Very useful	Useful	Not useful
Effective revision and revision plan	☐	☐	☐
Exam guidance			
Websites and mindmaps			
Preparation questions	☐	☐	☐
Exam standard questions	☐	☐	☐
'Pass Marks' section in answers	☐	☐	☐
Content and structure of answers	☐	☐	☐
Marking schemes	☐	☐	☐
'Plan of attack'	☐	☐	☐
Mock exam answers	☐	☐	☐

	Excellent	Good	Adequate	Poor
Overall opinion of this Kit	☐	☐	☐	☐

Do you intend to continue using BPP products?   ☐ Yes   ☐ No

Please note any further comments and suggestions/errors on the reverse of this page. The BPP author of this edition can be e-mailed at: suedexter@bpp.com

Please return this form to: Katy Hibbert, ACCA range manager, BPP Professional Education, FREEPOST, London, W12 8BR

REVIEW FORM & FREE PRIZE DRAW (continued)

Please note any further comments and suggestions/errors below.

FREE PRIZE DRAW RULES

1   Closing date for 31 July 2003 draw is 30 June 2003. Closing date for 31 January 2004 draw is 31 December 2003.

2   Restricted to entries with UK and Eire addresses only. BPP employees, their families and business associates are excluded.

3   No purchase necessary. Entry forms are available upon request from BPP Professional Education. No more than one entry per title, per person. Draw restricted to persons aged 16 and over.

4   Winners will be notified by post and receive their cheques not later than 6 weeks after the relevant draw date.

5   The decision of the promoter in all matters is final and binding. No correspondence will be entered into.